Patrice-Anne Rutledge

Sams **Teach Yourself**

LinkedIn®

in **10 Minutes**

Second Edition

SAMS | 800 East 96th Street, Indianapolis, Indiana 46240

Sams Teach Yourself LinkedIn® in 10 Minutes, Second Edition

Copyright © 2011 by Sams Publishing

ISBN-13: 978-0-672-33544-0

ISBN-10: 0-672-33544-1

Library of Congress Cataloging-in-Publication data is on file.

Printed in the United States of America

First printing February 2011

Trademarks

All terms mentioned in this book that are known to be trademarks or service marks have been appropriately capitalized. Sams Publishing cannot attest to the accuracy of this information. Use of a term in this book should not be regarded as affecting the validity of any trademark or service mark.

Warning and Disclaimer

Bulk Sales

Sams Publishing offers excellent discounts on this book when ordered in quantity for bulk purchases or special sales. For more information, please contact

U.S. Corporate and Government Sales

1-800-382-3419

corpsales@pearsontechgroup.com

For sales outside of the U.S., please contact

International Sales

international@pearson.com

Associate Publisher
Greg Wiegand

Acquisitions Editor
Michelle Newcomb

Development Editor
The Wordsmithery LLC

Managing Editor
Sandra Schroeder

Project Editor
Seth Kerney

Copy Editor
Mike Henry

Indexer
Larry Sweazy

Proofreader
Apostrophe Editing Services

Technical Editor
Vince Averello

Publishing Coordinator
Cindy Teeters

Book Designer
Anne Jones

Composition
Mark Shirar

Contents

About the Author

Patrice-Anne Rutledge is a business technology author and expert who has been featured on CNN.com, AOL, CareerBuilder, Inc.com, Fox News, MSN, and other media outlets around the world. She specializes in teaching others to maximize the power of new technologies such as social media and online collaboration to promote their businesses and careers. Patrice is a long-time LinkedIn member and social networking advocate who uses LinkedIn to develop her business, find clients, recruit staff, and much more. Her other books include *Using LinkedIn*, *Using Facebook*, and *The Truth About Profiting from Social Networking*, all from Pearson. She can be reached through her website at www.patricerutledge.com.

Dedication

To my family, with thanks for their ongoing support and encouragement.

Acknowledgments

Special thanks to Michelle Newcomb, Charlotte Kughen, Vince Averello, Sandra Schroeder, Mike Henry, and Seth Kerney for their feedback, suggestions, and attention to detail.

We Want to Hear from You!

As the reader of this book, *you* are our most important critic and commentator. We value your opinion and want to know what we're doing right, what we could do better, what areas you'd like to see us publish in, and any other words of wisdom you're willing to pass our way.

You can email or write me directly to let me know what you did or didn't like about this book—as well as what we can do to make our books stronger.

Please note that I cannot help you with technical problems related to the topic of this book, and that due to the high volume of mail I receive, I might not be able to reply to every message.

When you write, please be sure to include this book's title and author as well as your name and phone or email address. I will carefully review your comments and share them with the author and editors who worked on the book.

Email: consumer@samspublishing.com

Mail: Greg Wiegand
        Associate Publisher
        Sams Publishing
        800 East 96th Street
        Indianapolis, IN 46240 USA

Reader Services

Visit our website and register this book at
www.informit.com/title/9780672335440 for convenient access to any
updates, downloads, or errata that might be available for this book.

Introduction

Although professionals have always acknowledged the value of networking, today's economic climate makes developing a solid network even more critical. LinkedIn, the leading social networking site for professionals, is the ideal tool for maximizing the potential of an online network. LinkedIn has more than 85 million members worldwide, including executives from all Fortune 500 firms and President Barack Obama. A new member joins approximately every second.

It's clear that today's technology has forever changed the way people find a job, promote their businesses, foster strategic partnerships, and develop their professional networks. But technology is just the enabler. The fundamental concepts of professional networking remain the same both online and off. Building relationships through mutual connections and trust is the foundation of success on LinkedIn just as it is in the real world.

Sams Teach Yourself LinkedIn in 10 Minutes, Second Edition is designed to get you up and running on LinkedIn as quickly as possible. This book focuses on standard LinkedIn functionality. LinkedIn rolls out beta functionality and new features on a regular basis, so the features available to you might vary at any given time. The companion website to this book will help keep you updated on what's new with LinkedIn. For now, turn to Lesson 1, "Introducing LinkedIn," to get started with this powerful networking tool.

Who Is This Book For?

This book is for you if...

▶ You're new to LinkedIn and want to become productive as quickly as possible.

▶ You want to find a job or promote your business online, taking advantage of all that social networking has to offer.

▶ You want to become productive on LinkedIn as quickly as possible and are short on time.

Companion Websites

This book has a companion website online at http://www.patricerutledge.com/books/linkedin.

Additional information is located at http://www.informit.com/store/product.aspx?isbn=0672330857. Here you can find additional lessons and articles, including information about recruiting job candidates, working with company profiles, advertising on LinkedIn, and using LinkedIn on your mobile device.

Conventions Used in This Book

The Sams Teach Yourself series has several unique elements that help you as you learn more about LinkedIn. These include

NOTE: A note presents interesting pieces of information related to the discussion.

TIP: A tip offers advice or teaches an easier way to do something.

CAUTION: A caution advises you about potential problems and helps you steer clear of disaster.

PLAIN ENGLISH: Plain English sidebars provide clear definitions of new, essential terms.

LESSON 1

Introducing LinkedIn

In this lesson, you learn the basics of LinkedIn and develop a strategy for success with this popular social networking site.

Understanding What LinkedIn Can Do for You

LinkedIn (www.linkedin.com) is the world's leading social networking site for business, with profiles of more than 85 million professionals around the world. LinkedIn is also rapidly expanding: A new member joins approximately every second. The site is extremely active with recruiters from recruiting firms as well as from major companies such as Microsoft, eBay, and L'Oréal, which makes it a prime hunting ground for job seekers.

Everyone from top CEOs to President Barack Obama has a LinkedIn profile. If you want to network for business on just one social networking site, LinkedIn is the site to choose.

Creating a professional profile and developing a solid network of connections on LinkedIn can help you meet many goals. For example, participation on LinkedIn can enable you to do the following:

- ▶ Find a job or recruit quality job candidates

- ▶ Develop your business by connecting with clients and partners and promoting yourself as a service provider

- ▶ Brand yourself online with a professional presence that demonstrates your expertise

NOTE: **LinkedIn History**

LinkedIn was founded in May 2003 when the five company founders invited 350 of their closest business contacts to join. By the end of that first year, LinkedIn had reached 81,000 members.

Understanding the Key to Success on LinkedIn

The key to success on LinkedIn is to establish clear goals and ensure that all your actions on the site work to achieve those goals.

For example, if your goal is to find a job on LinkedIn, you want to create a strong profile with keywords that attract recruiters. You also want to develop a solid network of professional contacts in your industry—the type of people who might hire you or who might provide relevant job leads.

On the other hand, if your goal is to find business leads and develop your platform as an expert in your field, you could use a different approach. A strong profile and network are still important, but you might also want to participate in LinkedIn Answers and LinkedIn Groups to promote your expertise among LinkedIn's millions of members.

Before establishing your goals, however, you need to understand the unwritten rules of LinkedIn. LinkedIn's focus is on developing a mutually beneficial online business network. With LinkedIn, you can stay in touch with your existing contacts and connect with other professionals who share your goals and interests. LinkedIn is not the place to amass thousands of "followers," engage in heavy sales tactics, or send spam-like communications. Keeping these rules in mind will help you develop a LinkedIn strategy that generates positive results in your professional career.

TIP: **Focus on Strategy, Not Filling Out Forms**

At first glance, LinkedIn appears deceptively simple. Its true power, however, comes from employing the strategic best practices of online networking, not on your ability to enter your professional data in a form.

Understanding LinkedIn Account Types

LinkedIn offers several account types, including a free basic account, four types of premium accounts, and three types of Job Seeker accounts. All accounts offer the ability to create a professional profile, develop a network of contacts, search for jobs and people, receive unlimited InMail and requests for introductions, participate in groups, and participate in LinkedIn Answers.

See Lesson 9, "Finding a Job," for more information about Job Seeker accounts.

PLAIN ENGLISH: **InMail**

An InMail is a private message from a LinkedIn member who is not your connection. Although you can receive InMail free if you indicate that you are open to receiving InMail messages, you cannot send InMail unless you pay for that particular service. InMail is a paid service because messages you send via InMail are far less likely to be confused for spam. Keep in mind, however, that InMail isn't the same as the free messages you are able to exchange with your connections after you have already made a connection.

PLAIN ENGLISH: **Introduction**

A LinkedIn introduction provides a way to reach out to people who are connected to your connections. By requesting an introduction through someone you already know, that person can introduce you to the person you're trying to reach. For example, one of your connections might be connected to a hiring manager at a company you want to work for. Requesting an introduction to this hiring manager is a much better way to find a job than just sending a resume along with hundreds of other people.

See Lesson 6, "Communicating with Other LinkedIn Members," for more information about messages, InMail, and introductions.

Using a LinkedIn Free Account

LinkedIn's free account offers so many powerful features that it should suit the needs of most users. Unless you specifically need a premium feature, try out the free account first before making the decision to upgrade. With a free Basic account, you can request a maximum of five introductions at one time, view 100 results per search, and save a maximum of three searches with weekly email alerts.

NOTE: **LinkedIn Is a Powerful Search Tool**

You can perform and save targeted searches for people, jobs, companies, and other LinkedIn content. See Lesson 7, "Searching on LinkedIn," for more information about LinkedIn search capabilities.

Exploring LinkedIn Premium Accounts

Premium accounts offer you the ability to contact more people who aren't connected to you and are ideally suited to recruiters or people using LinkedIn as a business development tool.

LinkedIn's premium accounts enable you to

- ▶ Perform unlimited one-click reference searches

- ▶ Receive an OpenLink Network membership

- ▶ Send unlimited OpenLink messages

- ▶ Access the complete list of who's viewed your profile

- ▶ View expanded profiles of everyone on LinkedIn, even people outside your network

- ▶ Receive LinkedIn customer service responses within one business day

PLAIN ENGLISH: **OpenLink Network**

The OpenLink Network is a LinkedIn premium feature that enables network members to contact each other without incurring additional fees.

Your choice of the specific premium account that's right for you depends on your needs for InMail, introductions, and searches.

The Business account costs U.S. $24.95 per month. With this account, you can

- ▶ Send three InMails per month
- ▶ Save five searches and receive weekly alerts on each
- ▶ Maintain 15 pending introductions at one time
- ▶ Create five Profile Organizer folders
- ▶ View 300 results per search

The Business Plus account is priced at U.S. $49.95 per month. With this account, you can

- ▶ Send 10 InMails per month
- ▶ Save seven searches and receive weekly alerts on each
- ▶ Maintain 25 pending introductions at one time
- ▶ Create 25 Profile Organizer folders
- ▶ View 500 results per search

The Executive account is priced at U.S. $99.95 per month. With this account, you can

- ▶ Send 25 InMails per month
- ▶ Save 10 searches and receive daily alerts on each

▶ Maintain 35 pending introductions at one time

▶ Create 50 Profile Organizer folders

▶ View the full name of your 3rd degree connections

▶ View 700 results per search

The Pro account, at U.S. $499.95 per month, might interest power users. Pro users can

▶ Send 50 InMails per month

▶ Save 15 searches and receive daily alerts on each

▶ Maintain 50 pending introductions at one time

▶ Create 75 Profile Organizer folders

▶ View the full name of your 3rd degree connections

▶ View 1,000 results per search

NOTE: **Get More with LinkedIn Talent Advantage**

If you need a higher volume of InMails and introductions than the available premium accounts offer, consider signing up for LinkedIn Talent Advantage (talent.linkedin.com), a suite of power solutions for recruiters.

Creating a LinkedIn Account

Signing up for a LinkedIn account is a simple, straightforward task. Figure 1.1 shows the welcome screen that greets you the first time you visit LinkedIn (www.linkedin.com).

To create your own LinkedIn account, follow these steps:

1. In the Join LinkedIn Today box, enter your first name, last name, email address, and a password. Be sure to create a strong password. A password that contains a combination of uppercase and lowercase letters, numbers, and symbols provides the most protection.

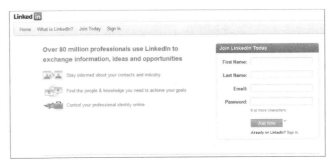

FIGURE 1.1   You can quickly sign up for your own free account from LinkedIn's home page.

TIP: **Choose the Right Email Address**

LinkedIn offers privacy controls to protect your business email address. Entering the email address that most of your business contacts use to communicate with you yields the best results when others try to connect with you by email on LinkedIn.

---

2. Click the Join Now button. The Let's Get Your Professional Profile Started page appears, shown in Figure 1.2.

3. In the I Am Currently field, select your employment status from the options available: Employed, A Business Owner, Looking for Work, Working Independently, or a Student. The selection you make in this field affects which additional fields display on this page. In this example, we'll use the fields that display if you specify that you're employed. If you select another status, the field you see will differ.

4. Enter your Country and ZIP or Postal Code. Note that LinkedIn displays only your geographic region, such as San Francisco Bay Area, and not your actual code or city on your profile.

Linked in ®

Everett, Let's get your professional profile started

I am currently:	Employed ▾
* Country:	United States ▾
* ZIP Code:	92606
	e.g. 94043 (Only your region will be public, not your ZIP code)
* Company:	Ning Consulting
* Industry:	Professional Training & Coaching ▾
* Job Title:	Business Coach

Create my profile

* Indicates required field.

FIGURE 1.2   Enter your basic data to get started on LinkedIn.

5. Enter your Company. As you start typing, LinkedIn locates potential company matches from existing profiles. Choosing from an existing entry helps ensure that you and your colleagues are correctly linked by company.

6. If LinkedIn doesn't find an existing match for the company you enter, the Industry field appears. Select the Industry that best describes your professional expertise from a list of more than 100 options. These options range from popular professions (Accounting, Banking, Computer Software, Internet, Real Estate, and Marketing) to the more obscure (Dairy, Gambling & Casinos, Fishery, and Think Tanks).

7. Enter your job title.

8. Click the Create My Profile button to open the See Who You Already Know on LinkedIn page. This page encourages you to search for and connect with people you already know. However, I recommend that you create your profile before completing this step. Why? Because when your contacts receive your connection

request, you want them to view a complete profile, not an empty one. To bypass this task for now, click the Skip This Step link.

9. Next, LinkedIn prompts you to confirm your email address. What displays on this page varies based on the email provider you use. Complete the verification process based on the prompts LinkedIn provides you.

> NOTE: **Understand the Email Verification Process**
>
> As a security measure, LinkedIn needs to verify the email address you entered when you signed up for an account. This ensures that the person who actually owns an email account, and not an impostor, signed up for LinkedIn.

10. The Do You Know These People page displays information about several people LinkedIn thinks you might know. Again, I recommend that you click the Skip This Step link and send invitations after you've created your profile.

11. On the You're Almost Done page, you can enter the email addresses of other people you know. Click the Skip This Step link to send your invitations after you've created your profile.

12. On the Your Account is Set Up—Choose Your Plan Level page (see Figure 1.3), you can choose to start with a free basic account or upgrade immediately to a premium account. Unless you're certain that you need the features offered with a premium account, I suggest that you start with the free account. To do so, click the Choose Basic button.

LinkedIn displays your home page (see Figure 1.4), welcoming you to the site.

> TIP: **Stay Logged In to LinkedIn**
>
> Now that you have a LinkedIn account, click the Sign In link whenever you visit the site to log on again with your primary email address and password. If you forget your password, click the Forgot

Password? link on the Sign In to LinkedIn page to request a new one. If you always use the same computer to access LinkedIn, such as a home computer, you can remain logged in for up to 24 hours as a convenience.

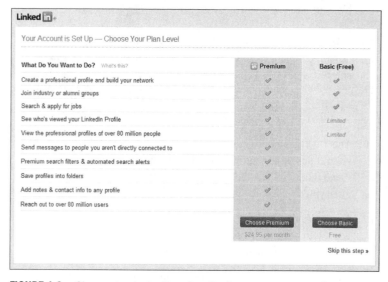

FIGURE 1.3   Choose to start with a free Basic account or upgrade immediately to access premium features.

FIGURE 1.4   Your home page is your main LinkedIn dashboard.

Exploring the LinkedIn Home Page

When you first create a LinkedIn account, your home page (refer to Figure 1.4) displays minimal content, which is understandable considering that you don't have any contacts yet. A welcome box greets you, encouraging you to search for and connect with people you know. Again, I recommend that you complete your profile before doing this.

It's important to remember that the content on your home page is dynamic and is unique to your LinkedIn actions, network, and account settings. After you start participating on LinkedIn, your home page changes. As an active LinkedIn user, the left column of your home page includes the following content:

▶ **Inbox:** Displays a preview of your Inbox with links to the three most recent unread messages. If you don't have at least three unread messages, the preview displays the number of unread messages that are available. See Lesson 6 for more information about your Inbox.

▶ **Network Activity:** Displays your current status and a text box for updating your status. See Lesson 5, "Managing and Updating Your Profile," for more information about updates. This section also lists recent activity from your connections.

> TIP: **View Your Network Updates as an RSS Feed**
>
> Click the Feed icon next to the Network Activity heading to open the LinkedIn RSS Feeds page where you can subscribe to your LinkedIn network updates and read them in a feed reader. See Lesson 4, "Customizing Your LinkedIn Settings," for more information on RSS and feeds.

▶ **Group Updates:** Displays recent group updates, including information about the groups your connections joined and comments and recommendations from fellow group members.

▶ **News:** Displays recent news articles about your company, competitors, and industry. You can also participate in discussions with your colleagues about news articles, recommend news to your colleagues, share news with your connections, or submit your own articles. Be aware that the News section appears on your home page only if news is available for your current employer. If you're self-employed or work for a small company, this section might not appear on your home page.

▶ **Just Joined LinkedIn:** Displays links to new colleagues and classmates who have joined LinkedIn recently.

TIP: **Customize Your Home Page for Easier Viewing**

To customize the network activity that appears on your home page, go to the global navigation bar, click the down arrow to the left of your name, and select Settings from the drop-down menu. On the Account & Settings page, click the Network Updates link to make your customizations.

The right column of your home page displays

▶ A list of three people you might know based on your existing connections. You can click the Connect link below their name to send an invitation to connect. If you haven't added any connections yet on LinkedIn, this option won't appear.

▶ A box with advertisements.

▶ The Who's Viewed My Profile? box, which tells you how many people have viewed your profile recently. To access details about who has viewed your profile, you must either allow others to view your name and headline when you visit their profile or upgrade to a premium account. If you haven't created a profile yet or no one has viewed your profile, this option won't appear.

▶ The Your LinkedIn Network box. This box lists your number of connections, the total size of your network, and the number of new people in your network.

▶ Boxes for LinkedIn applications and features, such as Events, LinkedIn Answers, Jobs, and Amazon Reading List recommendations. LinkedIn uses the information from your profile to determine relevant content to display. For example, if you select Marketing as your industry, the content displayed should be useful to a marketing professional. See Lesson 13, "Using LinkedIn Applications," to learn more about LinkedIn applications.

TIP: **Customize the Applications That Appear on Your Home Page**

To remove a box that displays in this column, click the X button in the upper-right corner of the box. Some boxes include an Edit link that you can click to customize the data that appears. To add application boxes, click the Add an Application button at the bottom of the column to select from the available options.

Navigating LinkedIn

Navigating LinkedIn is a straightforward process after you understand its navigational structure. LinkedIn pages display two navigation tools: a global navigation bar at the top of the screen and a bottom menu of additional options.

The global navigation bar, shown in Figure 1.5, includes links to the most popular LinkedIn destinations, with drop-down menus offering additional options. Links on the top navigation menu include the following:

▶ **Home:** Return to the LinkedIn home page.

▶ **Profile:** Edit or view your profile and recommendations.

▶ **Contacts:** Manage, add, and import connections.

FIGURE 1.5   LinkedIn's global navigation bar provides links to common tasks.

▶ **Groups:** View your groups, view a group directory, or create a group.

▶ **Jobs:** Perform an advanced job search or manage job postings.

▶ **Inbox:** View, send, and archive LinkedIn messages.

▶ **More:** Choose one of the following destinations from the drop-down menu: Companies, Answers, Learning Center, Upgrade My Account, and Get More Applications. This menu also includes links to your installed applications, such as Events or Amazon Reading List.

A search box appears to the right of the global navigation bar. See Lesson 7 to learn more about LinkedIn search options.

Above the global navigation bar, in the upper-right corner of your screen, you see a link to your name. Click this link to open the Edit Profile page. Click the down arrow to the left of your name to access a drop-down menu with the following links:

▶ **Settings:** Customize the way you use LinkedIn.

▶ **Sign Out:** Log off LinkedIn.

The Add Connections link displays to the right of your name. Click it to send invitations to potential LinkedIn connections.

The bottom of the LinkedIn screen provides links to additional menu options, including LinkedIn company information, LinkedIn tools, and premium features.

You learn more about these and other LinkedIn features later in this book.

Summary

In this first lesson, you learned about the many features LinkedIn offers, strategies for using the site, how to sign up for an account, and basic navigational tools. Next, it's time to create your profile.

LESSON 2

Creating Your Profile

In this lesson, you learn how to create a LinkedIn profile that generates results.

Viewing a LinkedIn Profile

Profiles form the foundation of LinkedIn. Your profile is your LinkedIn calling card, providing a quick snapshot of your professional background and experience.

Figure 2.1 illustrates a sample LinkedIn profile.

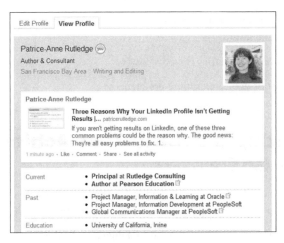

FIGURE 2.1   A solid profile generates positive results on LinkedIn.

A profile can include the following:

▶ A summary of your professional experience and specialties

- ▶ Your photo

- ▶ Your current status with comments from your network

- ▶ A list of the positions you've held and your major accomplishments at each

- ▶ A list of the educational institutions you've attended and your major accomplishments at each

- ▶ A list of the educational institutions you've attended and your major accomplishments at each

- ▶ Sections where you can list certifications, the languages you speak, your publications, patents, and specific skills you have

- ▶ Professional recommendations

- ▶ Data from LinkedIn applications such as your blog feed, Amazon reading list, shared presentations, attached resume, and more

- ▶ A list of your LinkedIn connections

- ▶ Information about your interests, association memberships, honors, and awards

- ▶ Your contact settings

- ▶ A list of your opportunity preferences

Creating a Profile That Achieves Your Goals

Before you create your profile, you need to think strategically about what you want to accomplish. Here are some tips for creating a quality profile:

- ▶ **Set goals for what you want to achieve on LinkedIn.** Are you looking for a job? Do you want to develop your business and find new clients? Are you a recruiter seeking passive job candidates? Make sure that everything you include in your profile works toward achieving that goal.

► **Make a list of keywords that relate to your experience, educa-tion, certifications, profession, and industry.** Every industry has its buzzwords, and you need to include these if they're terms a recruiter or potential client would search for. For example, an IT professional might include keywords such as Java, Oracle, SAP, or AJAX. A project manager might select PMP, PMI, UML, SDLC, or Six Sigma. A public relations professional, on the other hand, could choose PRSA, APR, or social media.

► **Have your current resume handy for easier profile comple-tion.** You can refer to it for any necessary dates or other data you might have forgotten.

CAUTION: **A Profile Isn't a Resume**

Remember, though, that a profile shouldn't duplicate your resume. A profile is a strategic summary of your professional background designed to achieve specific goals.

TIP: **Use the Box.net Files Application to Attach Documents to Your Profile**

If you really do want to include a resume on your LinkedIn profile, consider adding the Box.net Files application. With Box.net, you can share files such as PDF or Word documents on your profile. See Lesson 13, "Using LinkedIn Applications," for more information about Box.net.

► **Check for spelling and grammar errors.** Nothing detracts more from a good profile than numerous typos.

► **Remember that most people just scan your profile.** You need to capture their attention quickly and not overwhelm them with unnecessary details that detract from your goals.

► **Keep it professional.** A few personal details such as your inter-ests help humanize your profile, but too much emphasis on out-side activities also detracts from your professional goals.

> CAUTION: **Protect Your Privacy**
>
> Keep privacy issues in mind as you complete your profile. Enter only data that you're willing to share publicly.

Understanding Profile Completeness

To view your own profile, select Edit Profile from the Profile drop-down menu on the global navigation bar. The Profile page opens with the Edit Profile tab selected, shown in Figure 2.2.

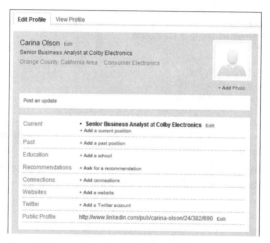

FIGURE 2.2   Create your profile on the Edit Profile page.

On the right side of your screen, you'll see a box that displays your profile completeness. It should be about 25% at this point, just for signing up for a LinkedIn account. This box displays a list of the additional percentage points you receive for completing specific tasks.

> NOTE: **How LinkedIn Calculates Completeness**
>
> You might notice that adding the listed percentages to your existing 25% still doesn't amount to 100%. That's because you need at

least two past positions and three recommendations to achieve
profile completeness.

To achieve a profile completeness of 100%, you need to complete the following items:

- ▶ Your current position

- ▶ At least two past positions

- ▶ Your education

- ▶ A profile summary

- ▶ A profile photo

- ▶ Your specialties

- ▶ At least three recommendations

Having a complete profile encourages people to network with you. In fact,
LinkedIn indicates that users with complete profiles are 40 times more
likely to receive opportunities than those with incomplete profiles.

TIP: **Move Beyond What a Computer Thinks Is Complete**

Just filling out the required fields to achieve 100% completion
doesn't guarantee success. You also need the right profile content.
A few words in a field might count toward a computer's view of
"completeness," but it won't be effective if your profile still contains minimal information.

Entering Basic Profile Information

Now that you have a plan for creating a solid profile, it's time to get started entering data. To add more content to the basic profile that LinkedIn
creates when you sign up, select Edit Profile from the Profile drop-down
menu on the global navigation bar.

The Edit Profile tab displays your name, title, company, location, and industry based on the data you entered when you signed up. Click the Edit link next to your name to open the Basic Information page.

The Basic Information page also includes several new fields. These include

▶ **Former/Maiden Name:** If you've changed your name at any point during your career, it could be difficult for former class-mates or colleagues to find you. Entering your former or maiden name makes it easier when people search for your former name.

▶ **Display Name:** By default, LinkedIn displays your full name. If you have strong privacy concerns, you can choose to display only your first name and last initial to anyone other than your own connections.

▶ **Professional Headline:** LinkedIn uses a combination of your title and company name as your professional headline, which should be sufficient for most people. You might want to customize this, however, if you're seeking work, are self-employed, or maintain more than one job. Some people include targeted keywords, pro-fessional certifications, or degrees in their professional headlines.

Some examples:

▶ PMP-certified IT Project Manager Seeking New Opportunities

▶ Bestselling Author, Coach, and Business Consultant

▶ Public Relations Executive, MBA, APR, Fellow PRSA

Make your changes and then click the Save Changes button to return to the Edit Profile tab.

TIP: **Let the LinkedIn World Know What You're Doing**

The Post an Update link on the Edit Profile tab prompts you to share information with your LinkedIn connections. You can enter something now or wait until you have connections who can actually view your updates. See Lesson 5, "Managing and Updating Your Profile," for more information about updates.

Adding Positions

Although you already entered your current job title and company when you created your LinkedIn account, you'll want to expand on that basic information. To do so, click the Edit link next to your current position on the Edit Profile tab to open the Edit Position page, shown in Figure 2.3.

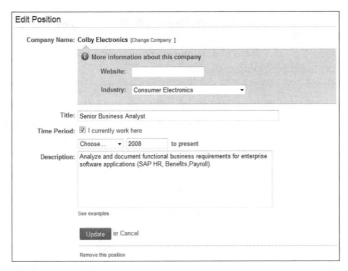

FIGURE 2.3 Let other LinkedIn members know about your professional success.

Enter a brief description of your current position, make any additional changes to the information you previously entered, and click the Update button.

Here are a few tips on what to include in the Description field:

▶ **Use keywords:** Think of the terms people would search for and use them in your description. For example, if you work in IT, mention actual technologies rather than vague generalizations.

▶ **Emphasize accomplishments over job duties:** For example, rather than say that you're responsible for sales, focus on your sales achievements and awards.

▶ **Be brief:** The Description field is a summary, not a detailed resume.

▶ **Keep your goals in mind:** If you want to attract recruiters, think about what would interest them in a potential candidate. If you're seeking clients for your business, focus on what would make them want to hire you.

NOTE: **Remove Positions You No Longer Want to Appear on Your Profile**

Click the Remove This Position link on the Edit Position page to delete that position from LinkedIn.

If you hold more than one current job, click the Add a Current Position link on the Edit Profile tab to add another current position. This is particularly useful for self-employed or independent professionals who have several income sources. For example, if you're an author, consultant, and blogger, you could choose to combine these activities under one position or create a unique position for each activity.

Add past positions by clicking the Add a Past Position link on the Edit Profile tab. Adding past positions is important because it provides a clearer view of your background and makes it easier to connect with your former colleagues at previous companies.

TIP: **Focus on the Last 10 to 15 Years of Employment**

If you have extensive experience, it's a good idea to focus only on the past 10 to 15 years of your work life unless an early position in your career is very relevant to your current goals.

Adding Educational Information

Next, you'll add information about your educational background. LinkedIn uses this information to help you connect easily with former classmates.

Consider the following best practices when choosing what educational information to enter:

▶ Include colleges and universities from which you received a degree.

▶ Include *relevant* certificates and continuing education course-work. For example, if you're looking for a job in a new field and have completed a related certificate, you should include this information.

▶ Don't include every continuing education course or seminar you've ever taken. It's important to be strategic, not prolific.

▶ Don't include your high school information unless you're still in college, are a recent graduate, or specifically want to reconnect with high school classmates.

To enter educational information, follow these steps:

1. Click the Add a School link on the Edit Profile tab. The Add Education page opens, shown in Figure 2.4.

FIGURE 2.4   Provide a summary of your educational accomplishments.

2. Select your country (and state, if you're in the United States).

3. Select your school name from the drop-down list that displays. If you can't find your school in the list, scroll down to the end and select Other. You can then enter your school name manually in the Type School Name field.

4. Enter your degree, such as BA, BS, or MBA.

5. Enter your field(s) of study. This can be your major, an area of concentration, or the name of a certificate.

6. In the Dates Attended fields, enter the years you attended. If you're still a student, enter your anticipated year of graduation in the second field.

NOTE: **Deciding Whether to Include Graduation Years**

The decision whether to include your year of graduation is a personal choice for many experienced professionals. LinkedIn doesn't require you to list the year you graduated; this is an optional field. Keep in mind, however, that LinkedIn won't be able to automatically search for your former classmates if you omit your graduation year. You would need to perform a manual search for former classmates.

---

7. List relevant activities in the Activities and Societies field. This might include honors, study abroad, and any extracurricular activities.

8. Add any additional notes about your educational experience.

9. Click the Save Changes button to return to the Edit Profile tab.

NOTE: **Enter Only Relevant Information**

You don't need to complete all the fields on the Add Education page to provide an accurate picture of your educational background. For example, details about your participation with the ski club or theater groups 20 years ago won't add real value to your LinkedIn profile unless they relate to your current career. Entering the most pertinent data ensures that people who read your profile focus on what's relevant.

The next section on the Edit Profile tab, Recommendations, encourages you to request professional recommendations. My recommendation, however, is for you to first complete your profile and then add connections before requesting recommendations. See Lesson 10, "Requesting and Providing Recommendations" for more information about LinkedIn recommendations.

Adding Website Links and Other Additional Information

To list websites on your LinkedIn profile—as well as add other information about your interests and achievements—follow these steps:

1. Click the Add a Website link on the Edit Profile tab. The Additional Information page opens, shown in Figure 2.5.

FIGURE 2.5   Add links to your website or blog on your LinkedIn profile.

2. From the Websites drop-down list, select the type of link you want to add. Options include My Website, My Company, My Blog, My RSS Feed, My Portfolio, or Other. If you select Other, a text box appears in which you can enter the name of your choice.

TIP: **Gain Name Recognition for Your Sites**

You can use the Other option to gain name recognition for your site or blog. For example, if you have a blog called Project Management Best Practices, you might prefer to create a link with that name

---

rather than using the generic "My Website" or "My Blog." In addition, you can use this field to link to your business's Facebook page other social sites.

3. Enter the complete URL of the site you want to link to, such as http://www.patricerutledge.com.

NOTE: **You Can List a Maximum of Three Sites**

To avoid clutter and prevent link spam, you can enter only three websites on your LinkedIn profile. If you have more than three sites to consider, think carefully about which sites would generate the most interest on a business networking site such as LinkedIn.

4. In the Interests text box, enter a list of your professional and personal interests. Be sure to use commas to separate interests so this content is searchable. Each interest becomes a link on your actual profile that you can click to search for others who share your interests. Again, think about meaningful keywords for this section rather than lengthy descriptions.

5. List the groups and associations to which you belong. Use commas to separate this information as well because the terms also become searchable links on your profile.

6. List any honors and awards you've received.

7. Click the Save Changes button to update your profile and return to the Edit Profile page.

Integrating Your LinkedIn Account with Twitter

If you have an account on Twitter (www.twitter.com), you might want to consider integrating it with LinkedIn. By doing so, you can share selected Twitter updates.

To set up LinkedIn to integrate with Twitter, follow these steps:

1. On the Edit Profile tab, click the Add a Twitter Account link.

2. In the pop-up box, enter your Twitter username or email as well as your password. If you're already logged in to Twitter, LinkedIn skips this step.

3. Click the Allow button.

4. In the next pop-up box (see Figure 2.6), specify whether you want to share all your tweets in your LinkedIn status or only selected tweets. In general, it's a good idea to be selective in sharing your tweets on LinkedIn. If you're a frequent Twitter user, some of your tweets might appear out of context on LinkedIn. To share only specific tweets, use the #in or #li hashtag at the end of any tweet you want to post as a LinkedIn status.

FIGURE 2.6   Share your tweets on LinkedIn.

5. Click the Save Settings button.

To make changes to the way you integrate LinkedIn and Twitter, click the Edit link to the right of the Twitter field on the Edit Profile tab. On the Twitter Settings page, you can hide your Twitter username on your profile, change the way you share your tweets, remove Twitter integration, or add another Twitter account. See Lesson 4, "Customizing Your LinkedIn Settings," for more information about the Twitter Settings page.

You can also share your LinkedIn updates on Twitter by selecting the Twitter check box when you post updates (see Lesson 5). To further integrate your LinkedIn and Twitter accounts, consider adding the Tweets application to share your latest tweets on your profile and home page (see Lesson 13.

Customizing Your Public Profile

LinkedIn makes a public version of your profile available to all web users, regardless of whether they're LinkedIn members or connected to you. When someone searches your name on Google or Yahoo!, for example, the public version of your profile appears in search results. Although a public profile is a great way to promote your career and gain visibility, it isn't for everyone. Don't worry. You have control over exactly what others can view on your profile. You can even hide your profile from public view if you choose.

By default, your public LinkedIn URL looks something like this: http://www.linkedin.com/pub/patrice-rutledge/13/521/845. The numbers in this URL address aren't very user-friendly, however, so you'll want to customize your public profile URL to something easier to remember such as www.linkedin.com/in/patriceannerutledge.

To do so, follow these steps:

1. On the Edit Profile tab, click the Edit link to the right of your Public Profile URL. The Public Profile page opens, as shown in Figure 2.7.

FIGURE 2.7   Create a user-friendly URL for your LinkedIn public profile.

2. Enter the custom URL you prefer. Using your first name and last name as one string of characters is a good choice. Spaces, symbols, and special characters aren't allowed in your URL.

3. Click the Set Address button to save your changes.

4. In the Public Profile section, clear the check box next to any fields you do not want to appear on your public profile.

> TIP: **You Can Hide Your Profile from Public View**
> To hide your entire profile from public view on the web, click the None option button in the Public Profile section.

5. Click the Save Changes button to update your public profile.

6. Click the View My Public Profile as Others See It link to preview what your public profile looks like on the web.

Adding Profile Sections

LinkedIn enables you to add sections to your profile that share information about your certifications, languages spoken, patents, publications, and skills.

To add a section to your profile, follow these steps:

1. On the Edit Profile tab, click the Add Sections link. The Add Sections dialog box opens, shown in Figure 2.8.

2. On the left side of the box, select the type of section you want to add. Choices include Certifications, Languages, Patents, Publications, or Skills. In this example, we'll choose Skills, one of the most popular sections to add. Be aware that if you choose another option, the remaining steps will differ.

3. Click the Add to Profile button. Depending on your choice in step 3, a new LinkedIn page opens. Because we chose Skills, the Add Skills page opens. Figure 2.9 shows this page.

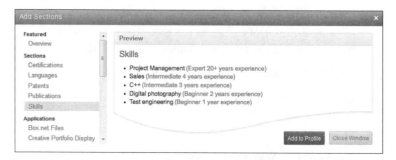

FIGURE 2.8   Add sections to your profile to share more information about your achievements.

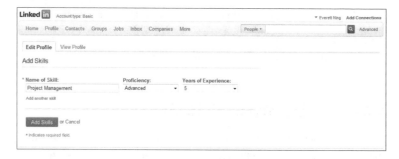

FIGURE 2.9   Let prospective employers and clients know about your skills.

4. Enter the name of a specific skill and select your proficiency level and years of experience from the drop-down lists. For example, if you're a project manager, you could list Project Management as one of your skills.

5. To add another skill, click the Add Another Skill link.

6. When you finish adding skills, click the Add Skills button to add your content to your profile.

After adding a section to your profile, you can edit or delete this content by clicking the Edit link next to the profile section.

Adding a Profile Summary

The next section on the Edit Profile tab asks you to enter a profile summary. This is an important step because people scanning your profile often read this section first.

To create your summary, follow these steps:

1. On the Edit Profile tab, click the Edit link to the right of the Summary heading. The Summary page opens, shown in Figure 2.10.

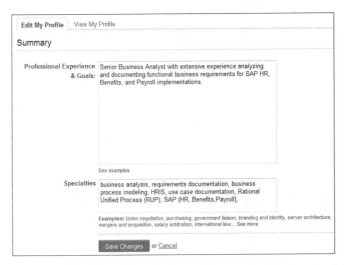

FIGURE 2.10   Provide a concise summary of your professional accomplishments.

> TIP: **Review Other Profiles in Your Industry**
>
> To get some ideas about what to include in your summary section, analyze the profiles of others in your profession or industry. Each industry has its own buzzwords and "personality," so what works for one professional might not be as appropriate for another.

2. Enter a summary of your professional experience and goals. In addition to summarizing your professional experience, you can also use this field to indicate that you're looking for job opportunities (assuming you're currently unemployed), recruiting staff, accepting new clients, or seeking new business partners, for example. Be sure to keep it professional, however. This is not the place for an advertisement or sales hype.

3. List your specialties in the Specialties in Your Industries of Expertise field.

4. Click the Save Changes button to return to the Edit Profile tab.

The next four sections—Experience, Education, Recommendations, and Additional Information—appeared earlier on the Edit Profile tab. You can click the Edit links in any of these sections to make additional changes, or you can continue to the next section.

Adding Personal Information

Near the bottom of the Edit Profile tab, you'll find the Personal Information section. In this section, you can enter the following data: phone, address, IM (instant message), birthday, and marital status.

If you want to add any of this information to your profile, click the Add link to open the Personal Information page. The Birthday, Birth Year, and Marital Status fields display a lock button next to them. Click this button to restrict visibility to only your connections or only your network.

CAUTION: **Consider Your Personal Privacy**

Entering any data in the Personal Information section is optional. Carefully consider your personal privacy before making any personal information public, even to a restricted group of people.

Specifying Contact Settings

Next, specify what types of messages you'll accept and what opportunities you're interested in. To update the Contact Settings page, shown in Figure 2.11, follow these steps:

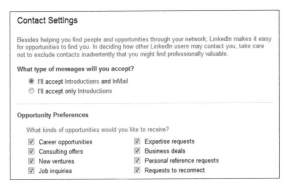

FIGURE 2.11   Tell other LinkedIn members about your contact preferences.

1. At the bottom of the Edit Profile tab, click the Edit link next to the Contact Settings heading.

2. In the What Type Of Messages Will You Accept? field, indicate whether you'll accept both introductions and InMail or if you'll accept only introductions. See Lesson 6, "Communicating with Other LinkedIn Members," for more information about InMail and introductions. In general, accepting InMail is a good idea if you want people you don't know to be able to contact you, such as recruiters.

3. In the Opportunity Preferences section, indicate the opportunities you're open to. If you're looking for a job or recruiting staff, for example, it's important to let people know this. Your options include

- ► Career opportunities
- ► Expertise requests
- ► Consulting offers
- ► Business deals
- ► New ventures
- ► Personal reference requests
- ► Job inquiries
- ► Requests to reconnect

FIGURE 2.12   Let a professional photo bring your LinkedIn profile to life.

4. Enter the advice you would give to members considering contacting you. In this text box, you can indicate that you're open to connecting with new people, you want to connect only with people you know, and so forth.

5. Click the Save Changes button to return to the Edit Profile tab.

Just below the Contact Settings section on the Edit Profile tab is the Applications section, which suggests several applications you can add to your profile. See Lesson 13 for more information about the many ways you can benefit from LinkedIn applications.

Adding a Profile Photo

Finally, you should add a photo to your LinkedIn profile. A photo helps bring your profile to life and sets you apart from other LinkedIn members. A professional headshot works best on your LinkedIn profile.

To upload your photo, follow these steps:

1. At the top of the Edit Profile tab, click the Add Photo link. The Edit Photo page appears, as shown in Figure 2.12.

2. Click the Browse button to open the File Upload dialog box. Depending on your browser or operating system, this dialog box could have a different name.

3. Select the photo you want to upload and click the Open button. Depending on your browser or operating system, the name of this button could vary.

> NOTE: **Photo Format and Size Limits**
> You can upload a photo in a JPG, GIF, or PNG file format. The file cannot be larger than 4MB.

4. Click the Upload Photo button. LinkedIn shows you a preview of how your photo will appear on your profile.

5. Use LinkedIn's resizing tool to make any modifications, and click the Save Photo button to complete the upload process.

6. Indicate your photo visibility preferences. You can specify that your photo is visible to your connections, to your network, or to everyone. Note that your connections include only the people you directly connect with; your network includes the people connected to your connections.

7. Click the Save Settings button to finish the upload and return to the Edit Profile tab.

TIP: **Easily Replace or Remove Your Photo**

If you want to replace or remove your profile photo, click the Edit link below your photo on the Edit Profile tab. Here you can upload a new photo or click the Delete Photo link to remove your photo.

Viewing Your Profile

To preview your profile, click the View Profile tab on the Profile page. Review all your entries carefully, checking for content accuracy as well as for grammar and spelling errors. If necessary, revise any of your entries by clicking the Edit link next to the item you want edit.

See Lesson 5 for information about keeping your profile updated, printing your profile, and promoting your profile on the web.

NOTE: **You Can Create Profiles in Multiple Languages**

If you speak a language other than English, consider creating a profile in that language as well. To do so, click the Create Your Profile in Another Language link on the Edit Profile tab (it's just below your greeting on the right side of the page).

Summary

In this lesson, you learned how to create a quality profile that should help you achieve your goals on LinkedIn. Next, it's time to start adding connections.

LESSON 3

Adding and Managing Connections

In this lesson, you learn how to develop a solid LinkedIn connection strategy, connect with other members, and manage your contacts.

Developing a Connection Strategy

After creating a strong profile, the next step in making the most of your LinkedIn experience is developing a solid network of professional connections. Before you add connections to LinkedIn, however, you should develop a connection strategy that matches your goals and networking philosophy.

> TIP: **Match Your Connection Strategy with LinkedIn Goals**
>
> In Lesson 1, "Introducing LinkedIn," you established goals for what you want to accomplish on LinkedIn. Be sure that your connection strategy helps you meet these goals. For example, if you're looking for a new job in a specific industry, your focus will be to connect with recruiters and other professionals in that industry. If your LinkedIn goal is to develop your business or build a platform, you might want to connect with a broader spectrum of people.

The three most common approaches are

- ▶ **Connect only with people you know.** LinkedIn members who follow this approach connect only with colleagues, classmates, and associates they personally know or who their known connections recommend to them.

▶ **Connect with people you know plus strategic contacts you would like to know.** With this approach, you connect with people you know and also seek out strategic connections who match your networking goals.

▶ **Connect with anyone and everyone.** Some LinkedIn members, particularly those who want to use the site for business development purposes, are open networkers and like to connect with as many people as possible and make special efforts to connect with thousands of people.

PLAIN ENGLISH: **Open Networker**

An *open networker* is a LinkedIn member who is open to connecting with people they don't know. Several LinkedIn groups exist for open networkers, such as LION (LinkedIn Open Networker) and TopLinked. Although it's a good idea to network with new people and develop a mutually beneficial business relationship, be careful not to abuse open networking by connecting indiscriminately just to amass a very large network. Don't treat your LinkedIn network as a numbers game.

Which approach is best? There is no one right answer for everyone. LinkedIn members have their own goals as to what they hope to accomplish on the site as well as their own networking strategies and comfort levels.

To get started, consider connecting with current and former colleagues, current and former classmates, friends and other acquaintances, and fellow members of professional associations.

Who to connect with beyond these obvious contacts depends on your connection strategy and networking philosophy.

Building Your Network

LinkedIn offers several ways to build your network. You can

▶ Import your webmail or desktop email contacts and search for them on LinkedIn.

▶ Search for current and former colleagues based on the companies listed on your profile.

▶ Search for current and former classmates based on the schools listed on your profile.

▶ Search for other people you know using LinkedIn's advanced search functionality.

▶ Send an invitation request to someone who doesn't use LinkedIn yet.

Keep in mind that you don't need to use all these methods to develop your pool of LinkedIn connections. For example, you might not want to connect with all your webmail or address book contacts. Or your webmail account might contain personal email addresses, not the email addresses your contacts used to sign up for LinkedIn.

Importing Webmail Contacts

If you have an email account with a popular webmail provider (such as Windows Live Hotmail, Gmail, Yahoo! Mail, or AOL), LinkedIn can import the email addresses of your web contacts.

To import webmail contacts, follow these steps:

1. Click the Add Connections link above the global navigation bar.

> TIP: **Alternative Method to Import Webmail Contacts**
> You can also import webmail contacts by entering your webmail address and password in the welcome box that displays on your home page.

2. In the See Who You Already Know on LinkedIn box, enter your Email and Password for the email account whose contacts you want to import.

3. Click the Continue button. LinkedIn imports the contacts from your webmail contact list and displays a list of these contacts, as shown in Figure 3.1.

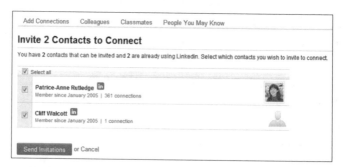

Add Connections   Colleagues   Classmates   People You May Know

Invite 2 Contacts to Connect

You have 2 contacts that can be invited and 2 are already using LinkedIn. Select which contacts you wish to invite to connect.

☑ Select all

☑ Patrice-Anne Rutledge 🔗
   Member since January 2005 | 361 connections

☑ Cliff Walcott 🔗
   Member since January 2005 | 1 connection

Send Invitations   or Cancel

FIGURE 3.1   Select the webmail contacts you want to connect with on LinkedIn.

> NOTE: **Connect with Imported Contacts Manually**
> Importing your webmail or address book contacts doesn't mean they automatically become LinkedIn connections. You must still manually choose whom to connect with.

4. Select the check box to the left of each contact's name you want to invite to connect on LinkedIn.

5. Click the Send Invitations button to send your invitations. Your contacts will receive your invitations to connect on LinkedIn and choose to accept or reject them.

> NOTE: **Confirm Your Email Address Before Connecting**
> You can't send invitations to connect until you confirm your email address. If you need to request a new confirmation message from LinkedIn, go to the global navigation bar, click the down arrow to the left of your name, and select Settings from the drop-down menu. On the Account & Settings page, click the Email Addresses link. Select the email address you want to confirm and click the Send Confirmation Message button. LinkedIn sends you an email with confirmation instructions.

Importing Contacts from Other Email Systems

Although LinkedIn imports webmail contacts automatically, you need to export your contacts from other email systems as a separate step. To do so, follow the instructions your email system provides for exporting your email address book data to one of the following:

- A comma-separated values (CSV) file, which is a computer file with a .CSV filename extension in which fields are separated by commas

- A vCard file, which is a file format with a .VCF filename extension, for electronic business cards

- A tab-separated file with a .TXT filename extension, which is a computer file in which fields are separated by tabs

LinkedIn accepts the following files for import:

- CSV files from Microsoft Outlook

- CSV or tab-separated files from Palm Desktop

- CSV files from ACT!

- vCard files from Palm Desktop

- vCard files from Mac OX X Address Book

To import a file exported from an email system, follow these steps:

1. Click the Add Connections link above the global navigation bar.

2. In the See Who You Already Know on LinkedIn box, click the Import Your Desktop Email Contacts link.

TIP: **Alternative Navigation to Import Email Contacts**
You can also import email contacts by clicking the Import Your Desktop Email Contacts link in the welcome box on your home page.

3. Click the Browse button to select the appropriate file on your computer. Depending on your browser or operating system, the name of this dialog box and button might vary.

4. In the File Upload dialog box, select the file you want to upload and click the Open button. Depending on your browser or operating system, the name of this dialog box and button might vary.

5. Click the Upload File button. LinkedIn imports the contacts from your webmail contact list and displays a list of these contacts (refer to Figure 3.1).

NOTE: **Resolving File Upload Problems**

If there is a problem with your upload, LinkedIn displays an error message and doesn't complete the import process. The most common reason for receiving an error message is that you tried to upload a file that isn't in one of the supported formats.

---

6. Select the check box to the left of each contact's name you want to invite to connect on LinkedIn. Be aware that importing your contacts doesn't mean they automatically become LinkedIn connections. You must still manually choose whom to connect with.

7. Click the Send Invitations button to send your invitations.

Connecting with Current or Past Colleagues

To connect with current or past colleagues, follow these steps:

1. Click the Add Connections link above the global navigation bar.

2. Click the Colleagues tab, shown in Figure 3.2.

3. Based on the current and past positions you entered on your profile, LinkedIn displays related company names and buttons that help you locate potential matches. Click the button that best matches the search you want LinkedIn to perform.

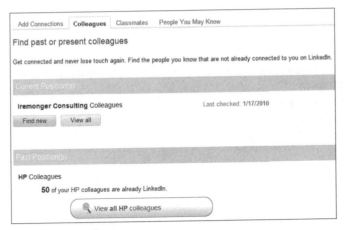

FIGURE 3.2 Connecting with your current and past colleagues is a great way to build your online network.

4. From the list of potential matches, select the individuals you know and want to connect with by placing a check box before their names.

5. Click the Send Invitations button to send invitations to these people.

> TIP: **Personalize Your Invitation**
>
> Select the Add a Personal Note with Your Invitation? check box to add a personalized greeting to your invitation to connect. Personalizing your request is particularly useful when reaching out to colleagues you haven't worked with in a while.

Connecting with Former Classmates

To connect with current or former classmates, follow these steps:

1. Click the Add Connections link above the global navigation bar.

2. Click the Classmates tab.

3. Click the link for the university you want to search from the list of schools from your profile.

TIP: **Search for Former Classmates from All the Schools You Attended**

If you didn't finish adding schools to your profile, click the Add Another School to Your Profile link to find classmates from additional schools.

---

4. View the search results and click the Invite link for the classmates you want to connect with.

TIP: **Revise Your Search Parameters for Better Results**

You can narrow or widen your search results by selecting View Graduation Year Only or View All Years Attended.

Connecting with Other LinkedIn Members

By now, you should have a good start on developing your LinkedIn network. Here are a few other suggestions for finding worthwhile connections on LinkedIn:

▶ **Review the list of people your connections are connected to, which displays in their profile.** It's very likely that you know some of the same people and would like to connect with them as well. View the profile of the person you want to connect with and click the Add [person's name] to Your Network link to send an invitation. For example, to connect with Felice Mantei, you would click the Add Felice to Your Network link.

▶ **Search for individuals by name in the Search People box on the top navigation menu.** Click the Add to Network link to the right of the person you want to connect with to create and send an invitation.

▶ **Search by keyword and location on the Advanced Search page to find local members of your professional associations.** Click the Advanced link on the top navigation menu to access this page. For example, you could search for the keyword PRSA (for the Public Relations Society of America) and the ZIP code 92606 within a 25-mile radius to find fellow PRSA members in Orange County, California.

▶ **Search for potential connections among the members of any LinkedIn groups to which you belong.** The Members tab provides a list of all group members with a link to their profiles. Remember, however, not to spam fellow group members with connection invitations. Be selective in determining who you want to connect with.

See Lesson 7, "Searching on LinkedIn," for more information on searching for people.

When you click the Add to Network link from any of these options, a page prompting you to create an invitation appears, shown in Figure 3.3.

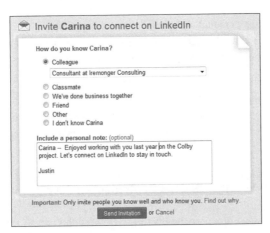

FIGURE 3.3 Specify how you know a target connection before sending an invitation.

To create an invitation on this page, follow these steps:

1. Select how you know your target connection from these options:

   ▶ **Colleague:** Select a company from the drop-down list that appears.

   ▶ **Classmate:** Select a school from the drop-down list that appears.

   ▶ **We've Done Business Together:** Select a company from the drop-down list that appears.

   ▶ **Friend**

   ▶ **Groups:** Select a LinkedIn group from the drop-down list that appears.

   ▶ **Other:** Enter the person's email address.

   ▶ **I Don't Know [First Name]**

> NOTE: **Add Connections Page Variations**
>
> If you haven't completed your profile data, you might see only a text box to enter your target connection's email address on this page.

2. Include a personal note in the text box explaining why you want to connect on LinkedIn. This is particularly important if you don't know the person you want to connect with.

3. Click the Send Invitation button to send your invitation to connect.

See Lesson 6, "Communicating with Other LinkedIn Members," for more information on viewing the status of connection invitations and other messages.

> TIP: **Consider Other Options for Contacting People You Don't Know**
>
> Two other ways of connecting with people you don't know are to send an InMail or request an introduction. See Lesson 6 for more information on InMail and introductions.

Connecting with People Not on LinkedIn

If you discover that some of your real-world networking contacts aren't using LinkedIn yet, it's easy to invite them:

1. Click the Add Connections link above the global navigation bar to open the Add Connections page.

2. In the Enter Email Address box (see Figure 3.4), enter the email address of the person or persons you want to invite. Separate multiple addresses with a comma.

FIGURE 3.4   Invite your real-world connections to join LinkedIn.

3. Click the Send Invitations button to send invitations.

Responding to Connection Invitations

In addition to sending invitations to connect, you might also receive invitations. To respond to an invitation, follow these steps:

1. Click the Inbox link on the global navigation bar to open your Inbox. If you have new messages, LinkedIn displays the number of messages in parentheses, such as Inbox (2).

2. Click the Invitations tab to view your open invitations, shown in Figure 3.5. Alternatively, you can also view new invitation requests in your Inbox preview on your home page.

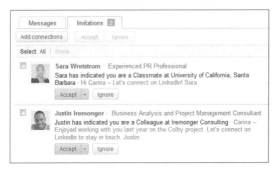

FIGURE 3.5   See who wants to connect with you on the Invitations tab.

NOTE: **Receive Invitations to Connect by Email**

If you specified that you want to receive invitations to connect by email on the Account & Settings page, your invitations also arrive by email. Click the link in the email to open the Invitations page.

---

3. If you would like to open the individual's profile, click the sender's name. Reviewing a LinkedIn member's profile can help you remember more about someone you don't know well or decide whether to connect with someone you don't know at all.

4. Take one of the following actions:

   ▶ If you want to add the person to your network, click the Accept button.

   ▶ If you want to send a message to the person who initiated the invitation before accepting or declining, click the down arrow to the right of the Accept button and select Reply from the menu. For example, you might want to ask why this person wants to connect before accepting.

► If you don't want to accept this invitation, click the Ignore button. LinkedIn moves this invitation to your Archived folder where you can view and respond to this invitation at a later time. After ignoring an invitation, LinkedIn provides two additional options: the I Don't Know [First Name] link and the Report as Spam link. Selecting the I Don't Know link blocks this person from inviting you again and alerts LinkedIn that this was an unwanted invitation request. Selecting the Report as Spam link reports the sender to LinkedIn.

CAUTION: **Think Carefully Before Clicking the I Don't Know or Report as Spam Links**

Because LinkedIn can penalize other users for sending too many requests to people they don't know—or for sending spam—think carefully before choosing these options. Selecting one of these options is too harsh if it's a genuine request from someone you just don't want to connect with.

When you accept invitations, LinkedIn adds those members as 1st degree connections in your network. You can add notes about the person and edit their contact information in the Contact Information section on the right side of their profile.

Managing Your Connections

After you develop your LinkedIn network, you need an easy way to find and manage your existing connections. The My Connections page offers several ways to do this.

Click the Contacts link on the global navigation bar to open the My Connections page, which displays a list of your connections (see Figure 3.6).

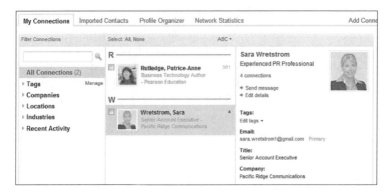

FIGURE 3.6   Find, contact, and manage your connections on the My Connections page.

Select a connection to display more information on the right side of the screen. Here you can click this person's name to open her profile, click the Send Message link to send a message on LinkedIn, edit details such as IM username or birthday, view an email address and work information, or enter tags that identify how you know this person. Clicking the Edit Tags link enables you to apply any of the following tags to a connection: classmates, colleagues, friends, group members, or partners.

If you have many connections, it might be difficult to find the person you're looking for. LinkedIn offers several ways to filter your connections. You can

▶ Hover your mouse over the ABC link to select a letter of the alphabet. LinkedIn displays only connections with a last name starting with that letter.

▶ Enter a keyword in the search box and then click the Search button.

▶ Narrow your results by tag, company, location, industry, or recent activity.

Removing Connections

If you decide that you no longer want to connect with someone on LinkedIn, you can remove that person as a connection:

1. Click the Contacts link on the global navigation bar to open the My Connections page.

2. Click the Remove Connections link in the upper-right corner of the page.

3. Select the check box next to the connections you want to remove.

4. Click the Remove Connections button.

People you remove are no longer able to view any data that can be viewed only by actual connections and they also can't send you direct messages. LinkedIn, however, doesn't notify them of the fact they have been removed.

CAUTION: **Remove Connections for the Right Reason**

Be sure that a connection really warrants removal before proceeding with the removal process. For example, if a connection you don't know well is bothering you with requests, spam, or sales pitches, this person is probably a connection worth removing. Removing former colleagues or associates simply because you haven't seen them in a while or don't work with them anymore, however, can be shortsighted.

Viewing Your Network Statistics

The Network Statistics page provides some interesting statistics about your network, including your total number of connections, the number of members you can reach through an introduction, the number of new people in your network, and much more. To view these stats, select Network Statistics from the Contacts drop-down menu on the global navigation bar.

Summary

In this lesson, you learned how to develop a connection strategy that suits your goals and started developing your own network. Next, it's time to customize your LinkedIn settings to give you the optimal online networking experience.

LESSON 4

Customizing Your LinkedIn Settings

In this lesson, you learn how to customize your LinkedIn profile, email, and privacy settings.

Customizing the Way You Use LinkedIn

Now that you've created a profile and connected with other LinkedIn members, it's time to customize your LinkedIn settings to optimize your experience on the site.

> TIP: **Customize for Optimal Privacy and Simplicity**
> If you're not sure which options to choose, select the ones that provide you the most privacy and simplicity while still allowing you to achieve your goals.

The Account & Settings page provides a lengthy list of options for customizing your LinkedIn experience. To access this page, go to the global navigation bar, click the down arrow to the left of your name, and select Settings from the drop-down menu. Figure 4.1 shows the Account & Settings page, which opens.

> NOTE: **Learn More About Account Options and Upgrades**
> The top portion of the Account & Settings page describes options for upgrading your account. See Lesson 1, "Introducing LinkedIn," to learn more about LinkedIn account options and upgrades.

FIGURE 4.1 The Account & Settings page provides numerous options for customizing your LinkedIn experience.

CAUTION: **Don't Skip Account Customization**

The many options provided on the Account & Settings page might seem overwhelming at first, and you might be tempted to skip this step. Setting aside some time to customize the options on this page, often a one-time task, can pay off in the long run. By customizing your LinkedIn settings, you'll better protect your privacy, receive only the specific information you want, and avoid any unpleasant surprises regarding the way LinkedIn handles your personal data.

Customizing Profile Settings

To customize your profile settings, go to the global navigation bar, click the down arrow to the left of your name, and select Settings from the drop-down menu. In the Profile Settings section of this page, you can customize the following:

▶ **My Profile:** Update and edit your profile content on the Edit Profile page. See Lesson 2, "Creating Your Profile," for more information about this page.

▶ **My Profile Photo:** Upload or remove your profile photo. If you don't want everyone to view your photo, you can restrict its visibility to only your network or only your connections. See Lesson 2 for more information and uploading and editing profile photos.

PLAIN ENGLISH: **My Connections Versus My Network**
Several of the options on this page give you the option to restrict visibility to My Connections or to My Network. *My Connections* refers to the LinkedIn members you connect with directly. *My Network* refers to the people two or three degrees away from your connections (in other words, your connections' connections). See Lesson 6, "Communicating with Other LinkedIn Members," for more information on this distinction.

▶ **Public Profile:** Specify the content you want to include in your public profile and customize your web URL.

▶ **Manage Recommendations:** Request, provide, and manage recommendations. See Lesson 10, "Requesting and Providing Recommendations," for more information about the power of LinkedIn recommendations.

▶ **Member Feed Visibility:** Make your member feed visible to everyone or restrict it to your network or connections. For maximum privacy, you can choose not to display your member feed.

▶ **Twitter Settings:** Enable your LinkedIn account to integrate with Twitter. If you've already added your Twitter account, you can change your access settings or disable the integration at any time. See Lesson 2 for more information about integrating LinkedIn and Twitter.

PLAIN ENGLISH: **Member Feed**
Your *member feed* refers to the network updates that appear on your home page and the home page of your connections.

Customizing Email Notification Settings

LinkedIn enables you to make extensive customizations to the way you handle email notification of various actions and activities. To customize your email notification settings, go to the global navigation bar, click the down arrow to the left of your name, and select Settings from the drop-down menu.

The Email Notification Settings section of the Account & Settings page lets you customize your contact settings, the way you receive messages, the invitations you receive, and the InMails you receive from LinkedIn promotional partners.

To customize your contact settings, such as the way you handle InMail and introductions, click the Contact Settings link. See Lesson 2 for more information on contact settings.

To customize how you receive messages on LinkedIn, click the Receiving Messages link. The Receiving Messages page appears, shown in Figure 4.2.

Receiving Messages

LinkedIn will send you a notification when you receive important messages from other users. How would you like to receive these notifications?

		Individual Email Send emails to me immediately	Daily Digest Email Send one bundle per day	Weekly Digest Email Send one bundle email per week	No Email Read messages on the website
General					
InMails, Introductions, and OpenLink	(?)	●	Not Available	○	○
Invitations	(?)	●	Not Available	○	○
Profile Forwards	(?)	○	Not Available	○	●
Job Notifications	(?)	●	Not Available	○	○
Questions from your Connections	(?)	●	Not Available	○	○
Replies/Messages from connections	(?)	●	Not Available	○	○
Network Updates	(?)	Not Available	Not Available	●	○
Referral Center Messages	(?)	Not Available	Not Available	●	○

FIGURE 4.2   LinkedIn enables you to provide specific instructions on its delivery of email messages.

You have four choices on the way you receive messages:

▶ **Individual Email:** LinkedIn sends an email to your primary email address as soon as the action takes place.

▶ **Daily Digest Email:** LinkedIn sends one bundled email notification per day.

▶ **Weekly Digest Email:** LinkedIn sends one bundled email notification per week.

▶ **No Email:** LinkedIn sends no email. You need to go to the website to read messages and notifications.

NOTE: **How LinkedIn Handles Bundled Notifications**

With bundled notifications, you don't receive a notification if there is no activity.

You can further customize your notifications based on message type such as InMails, introductions, OpenLink messages, invitations to connect, status updates, group updates, and so forth.

As you expand your network on LinkedIn, you could potentially receive a large volume of messages. Think carefully about how to best manage and process information. Many people choose to receive email notifications of the updates that are most important to them and review online those that are less time-sensitive. For example, you might want to receive invitations and job notifications immediately, but review group news only on the web. If you decide that your choices aren't working well for you, you can always modify these selections.

NOTE: **Notification Methods Vary by Message Type**

Not all notification methods are available for each type of message. For example, daily digest emails are available only for group notifications. Additionally, you can't receive network updates by individual email because this would involve more messages than most members want to handle.

To customize which connection invitations you receive, click the Invitation Filtering link. By default, you receive all invitations, but you can choose to receive invitations only from those who know your email address or those who are in your Imported Contacts list. Keep in mind, however, that restricting your invitations could block an invitation from someone you might actually want to connect with.

Finally, you can specify whether you want to receive InMail messages from LinkedIn marketing or hiring partners. To do so, click the Partner InMails link, and enter your preferences on the Partner InMail Settings page.

Customizing Your Home Page Settings

Network updates on your home page give you a quick snapshot of your connections' activities on LinkedIn. Although it's good to keep up with the latest news in your network, you might find that some network updates are of more interest to you than others are. See Lesson 1 for more information about your home page.

Fortunately, there's a way to customize exactly what appears on your home page. You can choose which updates you want to view and which you want to hide, including content from your connections, groups, applications, and more.

To customize your home page settings:

1. On the global navigation bar, click the down arrow to the left of your name, and select Settings from the drop-down menu.

2. On the Account & Settings page, click the Network Updates link in the Home Page Settings section.

3. Click the Manage Updates by Type tab, shown in Figure 4.3.

4. Specify how many updates you want to view on your home page. The default is 15, but you can choose from 10 to 25 updates.

5. Specify whether you want to Show or Hide each of the identified updates.

6. Click the Save Changes button. LinkedIn immediately makes the specified changes to your home page.

Show or hide updates
Control how many updates you would like to see on your homepage and which types you would like to see.

How many updates would you like to see on your homepage? 15 ▼

	Show Show on your home page	Hide Hide on your home page
General		
New connections in your network	⦿	⊙
Changes to your connections' status	⦿	⊙
Posts from your connections	⦿	⊙
Profile & Recommendations		
When connections change profile information	⦿	⊙
When connections change profile photos	⦿	⊙
When connections receive recommendations	⦿	⊙
When connections upgrade to a premium account	⦿	⊙

FIGURE 4.3   Customize the content that appears on your home page.

Subscribing to RSS Feeds

If you use a feed reader such as My Yahoo!, Google Reader, Newsgator, or Netvibes to subscribe to and read your favorite blog and news feeds, you might be interested in adding several LinkedIn feeds.

PLAIN ENGLISH: **RSS**

RSS stands for *Really Simple Syndication*, a popular format for web feeds. Content publishers can syndicate their content with a feed, making it available for users to subscribe to it and view with feed reader applications. Feeds for blog content are most common, but you can also create a feed for web content such as the content on LinkedIn. The advantage of feeds for the user is that you can view frequently updated content from your favorite blogs, podcasts, news sites, and other websites in one place. The standard feed icon is a small orange square with white radio waves, letting you know that the content is available via feed for your subscription.

To subscribe to LinkedIn feeds, go to the global navigation bar, click the down arrow to the left of your name, and select Settings from the drop-down menu. On the Account & Settings page, click the Your Private RSS

Feeds link in the RSS Settings section to open the LinkedIn RSS Feeds
page, shown in Figure 4.4.

LinkedIn RSS feeds

RSS is a technology that gives you access to LinkedIn content through your favorite RSS feed reader. LinkedIn offers two types of feeds, public and personal. Public feeds offer the same content to all LinkedIn members. Personal feeds contain private information from your LinkedIn network.

Network Updates
The Network Updates feed publishes your personal Network Updates in RSS format.

Important note about web-based feed readers
Some web-based feed readers publish your feed URLs on the web, making them available to search engines and everyone else. You should not subscribe to LinkedIn's Personal feeds with a web-based feed reader unless it guarantees that your feeds are kept private.

1. Turn on the feed for Network updates:
   Enable   Disable

Choose your feed reader or copy the link

or copy the RSS link:
http://www.linkedin.com/rss/nus?key=48P1i7BSi_Rrk
Generate a new RSS link for this feed

LinkedIn Answers
Each LinkedIn Answers category has its own public RSS feed.

1. Choose an Answers category
   Administration

2. Choose your feed reader or copy the link

or copy the RSS link:
http://www.linkedin.com/rss/questions?cat=ADM

FIGURE 4.4   You can view LinkedIn content with your favorite feed reader.

PLAIN ENGLISH: **Private Feeds Versus Public Feeds**

It's important to understand the difference between a private feed
and a public feed. LinkedIn private feeds contain personal data
such as your updates and your connections' updates and are
meant for your private viewing. Public feeds contain data available
for public viewing on the web, such as the content in LinkedIn
Answers.

LinkedIn offers a private feed of the network updates that appear on your
home page.

CAUTION: **Ensuring Feed Privacy**

Be careful not to publish your private feed on the web. If you use a
web-based feed reader, verify that your data will remain private if
you don't want others to view your LinkedIn network updates.

To subscribe to this feed, select the Enable option button and choose your
favorite feed reader from the buttons that appear. You can also copy the
RSS link and use it in another feed reader if you prefer.

Subscribing to public feeds of your favorite LinkedIn Answers categories is another option. Each category maintains its own feed, so you can subscribe to one or more feeds based on your personal interests.

To do so, select a category from the drop-down list and click the button for your preferred feed reader. You can also copy the RSS link to use it in another feed reader.

TIP: **Subscribe to LinkedIn News**

LinkedIn also offers an RSS feed for LinkedIn news updates. To access this feed, go to http://learn.linkedin.com/whats-new/ and click the orange RSS feed icon to subscribe with your favorite feed reader.

Customizing Group Invitations Settings

By default, you will receive group invitations from your connections. If you don't want to receive these invitations, you can block them.

To do so, go to the global navigation bar, click the down arrow to the left of your name, and select Settings from the drop-down menu. On the Account & Settings page, click the Group Invitation Filtering link in the Groups section to open the Group Invitation Settings page.

This page offers two choices for handling group invitations:

- ▶ **I Am Open to Receiving Group Invitations:** This is the default option that LinkedIn recommends.

- ▶ **I Am Not Interested in Receiving Any Group Invitations:** LinkedIn blocks all future group invitations, and you no longer receive them.

TIP: **View Group Invitations Only on the Web**

Rather than blocking all group invitations, you can specify to view them online rather than receiving them by email. See the section titled "Customizing Email Notification Settings," earlier in this lesson for more information.

The Groups section on the Account & Settings page also includes the Groups Order and Display link. See Lesson 11, "Participating in LinkedIn Groups," for more information on creating and using LinkedIn groups, including how to order and display them.

Customizing Your LinkedIn Personal Information

To customize your LinkedIn personal information, go to the global navigation bar, click the down arrow to the left of your name, and select Settings from the drop-down menu.

The Personal Information section on the Account & Settings page provides links to modify the following data:

- **Name and Location:** Update your name and location. Additionally, specify the display name you want others to see. If you have strong privacy concerns, you can choose to display only your first name and last initial (such as Patrice R.) to people who aren't your connections. Displaying your full name will yield better results.

- **Email Address:** Add or delete email addresses and specify your primary email address where LinkedIn sends all messages.

TIP: **Add All Your Email Accounts to the Email Addresses Page**
Enter all the email addresses you use on the Email Addresses page. This includes your work email, personal email, and school email if you're a recent graduate or still use a university email account. When people invite you to connect, LinkedIn matches the email address they enter for you to your LinkedIn account. Entering all your email accounts helps ensure a match.

NOTE: **The Importance of Confirming Your Email Address**
Remember that many LinkedIn features aren't available until you confirm your email address. If you haven't done so yet, or didn't

receive your original confirmation email, you can request another
confirmation message on this page.

▶ **Change Password:** Specify a new password to use. Changing
passwords on occasion is a good security measure. Also, remember to create a strong password that includes a combination of
uppercase and lowercase letters, numbers, and symbols.

▶ **Close Your Account:** Close your account and specify your reason for doing so. Keep in mind that if you choose this option,
you'll lose all your LinkedIn connections and will no longer have
access to the site.

Customizing Your Privacy Settings

LinkedIn enables you to specify privacy settings for the data you display on
the LinkedIn site and for the way LinkedIn uses your personal information.

TIP: **Read LinkedIn's Privacy Policy**

To learn more about LinkedIn's privacy policy, click the Privacy Policy
link on LinkedIn's bottom navigation menu.

To customize your privacy settings, go to the global navigation bar, click
the down arrow to the left of your name, and select Settings from the drop-
down menu. Next, click one of the following links in the Privacy Settings
section of the Account & Settings page:

▶ **Research Surveys:** Specify whether you want to receive invitations to participate in LinkedIn online market research surveys.

▶ **Connections Browse:** By default, LinkedIn allows your direct
connections to browse a list of your other connections. This can
provide a useful way to develop your network because it's quite

likely that you might know some of your connections' connections. If you want to hide your connections list, however, you can
choose to do so on the Connections Browse page. Your connections will still be able to view shared connections, however.

▶ **Profile Views:** The LinkedIn home page displays a box titled
Who's Viewed My Profile that provides information about the
people who visit your profile. You can customize what, if anything, LinkedIn publishes about you when you visit a LinkedIn
member's profile. Options include displaying your name headline, and photo; anonymous profile characteristics (such as industry and title); or nothing at all. If you're using LinkedIn as a business development tool, you might want others to know that you
visited their profile. Otherwise, you might prefer complete or
partial anonymity.

NOTE: **Your Choice in the Profile Views Section Affects
Profile View Stats**

Be aware that you must allow LinkedIn to display your name and
headline if you want to see who's viewed your own profile. If you
want to remain anonymous, you must upgrade to a premium
account to gain access to this information.

▶ **Viewing Profile Photos:** You can choose whose photos you want
to view. Options include all photos, no photos, or only photos of
people in your network or people who are your connections.

TIP: **Determine Who Can View Your Photo**

To specify who can view *your* photo, go to the Account & Settings
page, and click the My Profile Photo link in the Profile Settings section.

▶ **Profile and Status Updates:** When you update your status, modify your profile, or make recommendations, LinkedIn notifies
your connections of these changes and publishes them in company and industry updates. For most people, this provides good

exposure on the LinkedIn network. If you want to block these notifications, however, you can do so. LinkedIn handles profile update notifications and status update notifications separately, so you can choose to participate in one, both, or neither.

▶ **Service Provider Directory:** LinkedIn publishes a service provider directory for members who offer professional services. If another member recommends you, you can choose whether you want to be listed in the service provider directory. For most people, this is a great form of free publicity. If you're a corporate employee, however, you might not want to be included if you perform professional services only on occasion. See Lesson 14, "Using LinkedIn Service Providers," for more information about becoming a service provider.

▶ **Partner Advertising:** LinkedIn analyzes anonymous data from your profile, such as your industry, to customize the advertisements it displays and the content you view on partner sites (such as nytimes.com). For example, if you specify Banking as your industry, you'll view ads that are relevant to professionals in that industry. If you don't want LinkedIn to use your personal data in this way, you can opt out of this service.

▶ **Authorized Applications:** The Authorized Applications page enables you to remove LinkedIn applications you installed. You can also remove access to external websites that you previously allowed to access your LinkedIn data, such as Simply Hired or Business Exchange. See Lesson 13, "Using LinkedIn Applications," for more information about how to use LinkedIn applications.

Specifying How You Want to Use the LinkedIn Network

The final section of the Account & Settings page enables you to let LinkedIn know how you plan to use your LinkedIn network. For example, you can let LinkedIn know that you want to find a job, hire employees, sell products or services, and so forth. Click the Using Your Network link to provide LinkedIn with this informational data.

Summary

In this lesson, you learned how to customize your LinkedIn settings for optimal efficiency and privacy. This often one-time effort will pay off in the end with a much easier, more streamlined system for using LinkedIn.

LESSON 5

Managing and Updating Your Profile

In this lesson, you learn how to update your LinkedIn status and profile, promote your profile on the web, and print and download your profile.

Understanding the Importance of a Current Profile

Keeping your profile current is critical to your success on LinkedIn. Creating your initial profile might be a one-time task, but you need to update it regularly to let others know you're an active participant on LinkedIn. In addition to updating your actual profile, LinkedIn enables you to post frequent updates to inform your network about your activities and accomplishments.

Understanding LinkedIn Updates

LinkedIn enables you to share important news with other LinkedIn members in text updates of up to 600 characters. You can also insert URLs in your updates with a title, description, and optional photo. For example, you could link to your website, a blog post, or an article on an external news site. If you want to share your LinkedIn updates on Twitter, you should limit them to 140 characters. Otherwise, only the first 140 characters of your update will display on Twitter. Refer to Lesson 2, "Creating Your Profile," for more information about integrating LinkedIn with Twitter.

Figure 5.1 shows an example of a brief text-only update that's suitable for cross-posting on Twitter.

Figure 5.2 shows an example of an update that includes a link to a blog posting.

Sara Wretstrom Just received my certificate in Social Media Marketing from
the University of California, Irvine.
6 seconds ago · Comment · See all activity »

FIGURE 5.1   Quickly let your connections know what's new in your professional life.

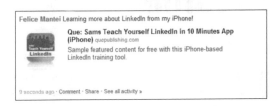

Felice Mantei Learning more about LinkedIn from my iPhone!

Que: Sams Teach Yourself LinkedIn in 10 Minutes App
(iPhone) quepublishing.com
Sample featured content for free with this iPhone-based
LinkedIn training tool.

9 seconds ago · Comment · Share · See all activity »

FIGURE 5.2   Showcase relevant blog posts with a LinkedIn update.

When you post an update, it displays in several places:

▶ At the top of your profile just below your name and headline

▶ In the Activity section of your profile, located in the right column

▶ In the Network Activity section of your home page

▶ In the Network Activity section of your connections' home
page—if you choose to share with them

Your update remains indefinitely until you either delete it or replace it with
a new update.

Although updates are a fun way to let your connections know what's new
in your life, they are also a strategic networking tool. Keep your goals in
mind and post updates that help achieve them. A well-crafted update can
be an effective marketing and publicity tool, but be careful to avoid overt
sales pitches in your updates. An update is a conversation with your network, not an advertisement.

Posting an Update

To post an update on LinkedIn, follow these steps:

1. On the global navigation bar, select Edit Profile from the Profile
drop-down menu.

2. On the Edit Profile tab, click the Post an Update link.

3. Enter your update in the box that appears, as shown in Figure 5.3. Remember that you can enter up to 600 characters unless you want to share your update on Twitter. In that case, you should limit your update to 140 characters (Twitter cuts off anything in excess of this length).

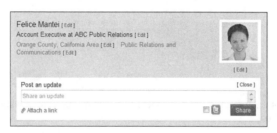

FIGURE 5.3   Post an update to let other LinkedIn members know what you're doing.

NOTE: **Alternative Method for Posting Updates**
Optionally, scroll down to the Network Activity section on your home page to enter your update in an identical box that displays there.

4. If you want to refer to an external URL, click the Attach a Link link. If not, skip to step 10.

5. Enter the URL you want to include in the Add URL box, such as http://www.quepublishing.com.

6. Click the Attach button. LinkedIn searches for this URL and displays a title, description, and photo from the content it finds on this page (see Figure 5.4).

7. Optionally, click the Edit link to make changes to this default content.

8. Enter any changes to the title or description in the text boxes. Remember that the description text displays in addition to what you enter in the update box.

9. The Include Photo check box is selected by default, but you can remove this check mark if you don't want to include a photo. To

change from the default photo, click the arrows below the photo
to view alternative selections. LinkedIn searches for any photos
on the page you're sharing and offers them as options.

FIGURE 5.4   Attach links to relevant external sites, such as a website, blog,
or news site.

10. Click the down arrow to the right of the Visible To drop-down list
to specify who can see this update. You can share with everyone
on LinkedIn or only with your connections.

11. If you set up LinkedIn to integrate with Twitter, you can select
the check box to the left of the Twitter button to share your
update on Twitter. If you haven't set up LinkedIn–Twitter integration yet, you're prompted to do so before continuing. Refer to
Lesson 2 for more information about setting up this integration.

12. Click the Share button to post your update, as shown in Figure 5.5.

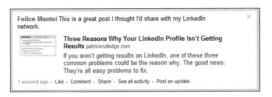

FIGURE 5.5   An update as it displays on your profile.

LinkedIn displays this update on your profile and home page. Your connections can also view this update on your profile and the Network
Activity section of their home pages. If you choose to share with everyone,

any LinkedIn member who visits your home page can view your updates, but your updates won't appear on their home pages unless you connect with them.

Managing Your Updates

After posting an update, you can

▶ Delete the update by clicking the Delete Your Update button (a large X) in the upper-right corner of your update box or in the [First Name's] Activity section in the right column.

▶ Share your update with groups you belong to or individual connections by clicking the Share link below your update. Figure 5.6 shows the Share dialog box, which opens.

FIGURE 5.6   Share your update with group members and individual connections.

▶ View a list of your latest updates by clicking the See All Activity
link below your update.

Commenting on an Update

When your update appears in your connections' Network Activity section
on their home pages, they can

▶ Enter their own comments by clicking the Comment link below
your update. If your connections have entered comments about
your update, you'll see a link beneath your posted update on
your home page and on your profile. The link tells you how
many comments you have (for example, 2 Comments). Click this
link to view your comments and add your own feedback to the
discussion.

▶ Send you a private message by clicking the Send a Message link.

▶ Show their support for your update by clicking the Like link.

▶ Share your update with their connections or fellow group members or in an update of their own.

> TIP: **Add Comments to Participate in the LinkedIn Community**
> Adding your own comments to your connections' updates is a good
> way to stay in touch and maintain visibility.

Updating Your Profile

Even if you create a thorough profile when you first sign up for LinkedIn,
you'll eventually want to update it with recent information.

You should update your LinkedIn profile whenever your employment status changes, you receive a degree or certification, win an award, learn a
new skill, start a new business, achieve a career milestone, or change your
LinkedIn goals. To update your profile, select Edit Profile from the Profile
drop-down menu on the global navigation bar. The Profile page opens with
the Edit Profile tab active, as shown in Figure 5.7.

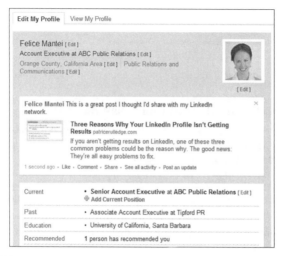

FIGURE 5.7   Be sure to update your profile regularly with new information.

The Edit Profile tab is the same place you first created your profile, so you should already be familiar with its content. After you first enter profile data, links such as Add a Past Position or Add a School disappear. Instead, click the Edit link next to any field you want to update. The appropriate LinkedIn page opens, where you can make any required changes.

Refer to Lesson 2 for more information about the content you can enter on the Edit Profile tab.

CAUTION: **Don't Let Your Profile Get Outdated**

Although it's not necessary to update your profile every week, you shouldn't let it get outdated either. If it's obvious that you haven't touched your profile in months, or years, LinkedIn members might not bother contacting you for what could have been a lucrative opportunity for you.

Promoting Your Profile on the Web

With your permission, LinkedIn makes a public version of your profile available for view and search on the web. Figure 5.8 shows a sample LinkedIn profile link in Google search results.

> **Patrice-Anne Rutledge - LinkedIn**
> San Francisco Bay Area - Author & Communications Consultant
> View **Patrice-Anne Rutledge's** professional profile on **LinkedIn. LinkedIn** is the world's largest
> business network, helping professionals like **Patrice-Anne ...**
> www.linkedin.com/in/**patriceannerutledge** - Cached - Similar

FIGURE 5.8   Your LinkedIn public profile appears in Google search results.

TIP: **Promote Your LinkedIn Profile in Print**

Although promoting your profile online is most common, many
LinkedIn members also print their LinkedIn profile URL on business
cards, brochures, and other marketing materials.

To customize the appearance of your public profile, go to the global navigation bar, click the down arrow to the left of your name, and select
Settings from the drop-down menu. On the Account & Settings page, click
the Public Profile link.

Lesson 2 provided details on how to manage your public profile. As a
reminder, here are tips to maximize your profile's online visibility:

▶ Customize your public profile URL to make it user-friendly, such
   as http://www.linkedin.com/in/patriceannerutledge.

▶ Select the Full View option on the Public Profile page and place a
   check mark next to all fields you want to appear on your public
   profile.

▶ Preview your public profile to ensure that you like how it appears
   to others on the web.

In addition to maintaining a public profile, you can also post a LinkedIn
button on your website, blog, or online resume. Figure 5.9 shows a sample
button.

Click the Customized Buttons link on the Public Profile page to open the
Promote Your Profile! page, where you can select the button style you prefer. LinkedIn offers a special button for TypePad users, but you can place
your button on any blog or website. For example, a blog sidebar is a great
place for a LinkedIn button. Copy the HTML code LinkedIn provides and
paste it into your own site.

FIGURE 5.9   Add a LinkedIn button to your website so that site visitors can view your profile.

Another way to promote your LinkedIn profile on the web is to include a link to your public profile URL in your email signature, on your online business card, or on other social sites such as Facebook or Twitter.

TIP: **Promote Your LinkedIn Profile on Facebook**
If you use Facebook (www.facebook.com), consider installing the My LinkedIn Profile application on your Facebook profile.

Printing and Downloading Your Profile

You can print and download your profile, or the profile of another LinkedIn member, by clicking one of the icons in the upper-right corner of a profile, shown in Figure 5.10.

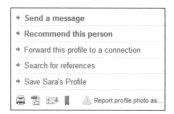

FIGURE 5.10   Print or download your profile using one of the icons.

Your options include

▶ **Print This Profile:** Opens the Print dialog box in which you can specify print options and print a profile.

▶ **Download as PDF:** Creates a PDF document from your profile that you can view with Adobe Reader (get.adobe.com/reader).

▶ **Download vCard:** Downloads your profile in the vCard format, which is a file format used for electronic business cards. This option appears only for your own profile or for your connections.

Summary

In this lesson, you learned how to update your status and profile, promote your profile on the web, and print and download your profile. Next, learn the many ways to communicate with other members and become part of the LinkedIn community.

Communicating with Other LinkedIn Members

In this lesson, you learn about the LinkedIn network and the many ways to communicate with other LinkedIn members.

Understanding Your LinkedIn Network

Before you start communicating with others on LinkedIn, you need to understand how LinkedIn classifies its members in terms of their connections to you. This distinction is important because it determines what, if any, restrictions LinkedIn places on your ability to contact people.

Your LinkedIn network consists of three levels of connections:

► **1st-degree connections:** LinkedIn members you connect with directly. Either you sent them an invitation to connect and they accepted, or you accepted their invitations. Your connection list on your profile displays your 1st degree connections. When LinkedIn refers to "your connections," this means your 1st degree connections.

► **2nd-degree connections:** LinkedIn members who connect directly with your 1st degree connections.

► **3rd-degree connections:** LinkedIn members who connect directly with your 2nd degree connections.

For example, if you connect directly with your colleague Nicole, she is your 1st degree connection. If Nicole connects directly to Ben, her former classmate, Ben is your 2nd degree connection. If Ben connects directly with Drake, one of his co-workers, Drake is your 3rd degree connection.

LinkedIn also considers fellow members of groups as part of your network. See Lesson 11, "Participating in LinkedIn Groups," for more information about LinkedIn groups.

PLAIN ENGLISH: **My Network**

Your LinkedIn network (termed *My Network*) differs from the entire LinkedIn network, which consists of all LinkedIn members. At the time of this printing, the entire LinkedIn network includes more than 85 million members.

TIP: **View Your Network Statistics**

To view how many people are in each level of your network, select Network Statistics from the Contacts drop-down menu on the global navigation bar.

Understanding InMail, Introductions, and LinkedIn Messages

LinkedIn offers several ways to communicate with other members. The type of communication you can send depends on how you're connected to these members. Your choices include

▶ **Messages:** Messages are the primary form of communication on LinkedIn. You can send messages to your direct connections as well as to the people who belong to the same LinkedIn groups as you do. If you can send a message to someone, the Send Message link appears next to their name on their profile and in search results. See "Sending Messages" later in this lesson for more information. Although you'll often see the term *message* used generically to refer to all items in your Inbox, it is a specific type of communication in itself.

▶ **Invitations:** An invitation is a request to connect with another LinkedIn member. Refer to Lesson 3, "Adding and Managing Connections," for more information about sending invitations.

▶ **InMail:** An InMail is a private message to or from a LinkedIn member who is not your connection. You can receive InMail free if you indicate that you are open to receiving InMail messages on the Account. In general, sending InMail is a paid LinkedIn feature unless the recipient is a premium member who belongs to the OpenLink Network. See "Sending InMail" later in this lesson for more information.

▶ **Introductions:** An introduction provides a way to reach out to the people who are connected to your connections. By requesting an introduction through someone you already know, that person can introduce you to the person you're trying to reach. You can contact your 1st degree connections to request introductions to members who are 2nd and 3rd degree connections. Members with free accounts can have up to five introductions open at a time. See "Requesting Introductions" later in this lesson for more information.

Understanding Your Contact Options

Before you start communicating with another LinkedIn member, you need to understand your available options for contacting that particular person. When you view member profiles or their summary information from another part of the site, the icons next to a member's name tell you how you're connected (see Figure 6.1).

FIGURE 6.1 The icons next to a member's name tell you how you're connected.

These icons identify 1st, 2nd, and 3rd degree connections; fellow group members; LinkedIn premium account holders, and LinkedIn OpenLink network members.

> NOTE: **Some LinkedIn Members Have No Icons**
>
> Members who display no icons next to their names are out of your network, don't share any groups, and aren't premium account holders.

The links that display to the right of a member's name let you know what contact options are available. These include

- **Send a Message:** Send a message to a direct connection or group member.

- **Send InMail:** Send an InMail to someone who isn't a direct connection. This option doesn't appear for members to whom you can send a message because it wouldn't make sense to pay to contact someone you can communicate with freely. If you click the Send InMail link and don't have a premium account, LinkedIn prompts you to sign up for one before you can proceed.

- **Send InMail (Free):** Send an OpenLink message to a member of the OpenLink Network. LinkedIn members who hold premium accounts can offer you the option of sending them free InMail. Refer to Lesson 1, "Introducing LinkedIn," for more information about the OpenLink Network.

- **Recommend This Person:** Post a recommendation for this LinkedIn member.

- **You Have Recommended This Person:** View the recommendation you posted.

- **Get Introduced Through a Connection:** Request an introduction to this member through a 1st degree connection.

- **Add [First Name] to Your Network:** Send an invitation to connect. Refer to Lesson 3, "Adding and Managing Connections," for more information about sending connection requests.

▶ **Forward This Profile to a Connection:** Forward a member's profile to a member you know, as a way of informal introduction.

▶ **Find References:** Search for LinkedIn members who worked at the same company at the same time as this member.

▶ **Save [First Name]'s Profile:** Save this person's profile to your Profile Organizer (a premium feature). See Lesson 7, "Searching on LinkedIn," for more information.

These are the link names that appear on an actual profile. The link names in search results are sometimes abbreviated.

CAUTION: **Not All Options Are Available for All Members**

Remember that you'll never see all these options for any one member. For example, it wouldn't make sense to send InMail, request an introduction, or add to your network a member who is already your connection, so these options don't appear for your connections.

Managing Your Inbox

Your Inbox is the focal point for all your direct communication on LinkedIn. A summary of your three most recent Inbox items appears at the top of your home page. You can also click the Inbox link on the global navigation bar to open the Inbox page, shown in Figure 6.2.

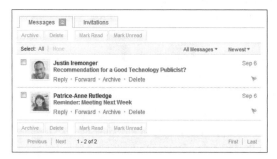

FIGURE 6.2   Your Inbox is the focal point for your personal communications on LinkedIn.

The default view of your Inbox is the Messages tab, which displays all the messages you've received. If you have a lot of Inbox messages and want to filter what you see, click the All Messages link and choose one of the available options from the drop-down menu. For example, you can choose to display only unread messages, flagged messages, InMails, recommendations, introductions, profiles, jobs, or blocked messages. By default, LinkedIn displays your messages in order from newest to oldest. To reverse this order, click the Newest link and select Oldest from the drop-down menu.

> TIP: **Search for Specific Content**
>
> In addition to filtering Inbox items, you can also search for a specific message. Enter a keyword in the text box on the left side of the page and click the Search button (the button with the magnifying glass). LinkedIn displays all messages containing that search term. For example, you could search for a person's name or a word or phrase in the subject line or message text.

From the Messages tab, you can

▶ View a pop-up box with information about the sender by pausing your mouse over the sender's name. To view the complete profile, click the sender's name.

▶ View a message by clicking its subject line.

▶ Reply to a message by clicking the Reply link below the message's subject line. See "Reading and Replying to Messages" later in this lesson for more information.

▶ Forward a message to another LinkedIn member by clicking the Forward link below the message's subject line.

▶ Archive a message by clicking the Archive link below the message's subject line. This moves your message to the Archived folder, which you can access at any time by clicking the Archived link on the left side of your Inbox. It's a good idea to archive old or resolved messages to keep your Inbox focused on your current action items.

▶ Delete a message by clicking the Delete link below the message's subject line. This removes the message from your Inbox and places it in your Trash folder. You can access the Trash folder by clicking the Trash link on the left side of your Inbox. In this folder, you can choose to empty your trash, undelete a message you deleted by mistake, or delete messages permanently.

TIP: **You Can Archive or Delete Multiple Messages**

To archive or delete more than one message at a time, select the check box to the left of all the messages you want to move and then click either the Archive or Delete button at the top of the Inbox.

▶ Mark a message as read or unread. By default, new messages appear in bold text to signify they have not yet been read. After you read a message, the message no longer is boldfaced in your Inbox. To change this, select the check box to the left of a message and click either the Mark Unread button.

▶ Flag a message as an action item for follow-up. By default, new messages include a flag icon to the right of the subject line, flagging it as an action item. Click the flag icon, which serves as a toggle, to flag or unflag a message for action.

The Inbox also includes another tab: Invitations. This tab displays all open invitations you need to respond to. Refer to Lesson 3 for more information about responding to invitations to connect.

Sending Messages

To send a message to a 1st degree connection or group member, follow these steps:

1. On the global navigation bar, select Compose Message from the Inbox drop-down menu. You can also send a message by clicking the Compose Message button from your Inbox.

2. In the To field, start typing the name of your connection and wait for LinkedIn to find a match (see Figure 6.3).

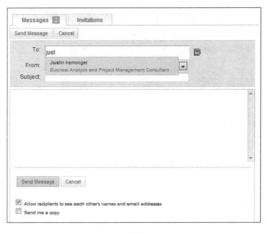

FIGURE 6.3   Sending a direct message to one of your LinkedIn connections.

TIP: **Send a Message to Multiple Connections**

Alternatively, click the address book icon to open your connection list. With the address book, you can search for the person you want to reach or select multiple recipients for your message. LinkedIn allows you to send a message to up to 50 connections at one time.

---

3. Enter a subject for your message.

4. Enter your message in the text box.

5. If you're sending a message to multiple recipients and don't want to disclose this information, remove the check mark before the Allow Recipients to See Each Other's Names and Email Addresses check box (selected by default).

6. To email yourself a copy of your message, select the Send Me a Copy check box. Your message already appears in your Sent folder by default.

7. Click the Send Message button. LinkedIn sends your message to the recipient and notifies you that your message was sent.

Although clicking the Compose Message link is the primary way to send messages on LinkedIn, you can also send messages by clicking the Send a Message link in a profile, on your home page, or in search results.

TIP: **Other Ways to Contact LinkedIn Members**

The profiles of your direct connections also display their external email address in the Contact Information box on the right sidebar. Some members include their email addresses directly on their profiles for the entire LinkedIn network to see.

Reading and Replying to Messages

You can open your messages from the Inbox preview on your home page or from the Inbox itself. (Access it by clicking the Inbox link on the global navigation bar.)

Click the subject line link of any message to open it. Figure 6.4 illustrates a sample message.

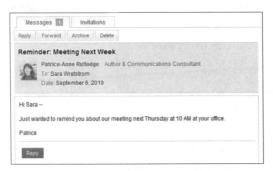

FIGURE 6.4   View a message and reply to it.

The buttons that appear at the bottom of a message vary depending on the message type and what actions you can take. For example, a basic message includes the Reply button, a recommendation request includes the Write a Recommendation button, and an invitation to connect includes the Accept button and Ignore button.

Sending InMail

As you learned earlier in this lesson, InMail enables you to contact LinkedIn members who aren't in your network. In an effort to manage spam, LinkedIn requires members to pay to send InMail. InMail is most useful for members who want to contact a wide variety of people, such as recruiters or individuals using LinkedIn for business development.

LinkedIn premium accounts, including Job Seeker premium accounts, enable you to send a fixed number of InMail messages per month. To learn more about LinkedIn premium accounts and InMail, click the Upgrade My Account link on the bottom navigation menu. To learn more about Job Seeker premium accounts, select Job Seeker Premium from the Jobs drop-down menu on the global navigation bar.

You can also purchase individual InMails at $10 each. To do so, go to the global navigation bar, click the down arrow to the left of your name, and select Settings from the drop-down menu. Then, click the Purchase link to the right of the InMails field on the Account & Settings page. This is cost-efficient only if you want to contact just a few people by InMail.

TIP: **When You Can Send Free InMail**

If you see the word *Free* immediately following a Send InMail link, you can send InMail to this LinkedIn member at no charge. To enable members to send you free InMail, you must participate in the OpenLink Network, a premium feature.

See Lesson 1 to learn more about the OpenLink Network and premium account options. See Lesson 9, "Finding a Job," to learn more about Job Seeker premium accounts.

To determine the InMail options available for a particular member, view the contact options on that person's profile (see Figure 6.5).

FIGURE 6.5   Determine the InMail options for a particular LinkedIn member.

> NOTE: **Where Is the Send InMail Link?**
>
> You won't see any Send InMail link for members who indicate on the Account & Settings page that they aren't open to receiving InMail. InMail isn't an option for your connections, either. You can contact them directly at no cost to either party.

To send InMail to a LinkedIn member, follow these steps:

1. Click the Send InMail link on the profile of the person you want to reach. If you're sending paid InMail, the Compose Your Message page opens. If you're sending free InMail, the Compose Your OpenLink Message page opens (see Figure 6.6). These pages contain identical information.

FIGURE 6.6   Sending free InMail to members of the OpenLink Network.

2. If you don't want to share your contact information with the person you want to reach, remove the check mark from the Include My Contact Information check box (selected by default). In general, it's a good idea to share contact information. To do so, enter your email address and phone number in the specified fields.

3. In the Category drop-down list, select the reason for your InMail. Options include career opportunity, consulting offer, new venture, job inquiry, expertise request, business deal, reference request, or get back in touch.

4. In the Subject field, enter the subject of your InMail.

5. In the text box, enter your message. To increase your chances of a positive reply, be as specific as possible.

6. Click the Send button to send your InMail. If the recipient doesn't respond to the InMail within seven days, the message expires.

For more information about InMail, refer to "Understanding InMail, Introductions, and LinkedIn Messages" earlier in this lesson and also refer to Lesson 1.

TIP: **Consider Alternatives to InMail**

Although InMail is an effective LinkedIn communication tool, it comes at a price. If you want to contact someone you don't know and don't want to pay to send InMail, you have several other options. You could join a group that this person belongs to and then send a message or invitation to connect as a fellow group member. You could also request an introduction through a mutual connection. Alternatively, you could choose to contact the individual outside LinkedIn by accessing the website links and external email information individuals provide on their profiles.

Requesting Introductions

Requesting an introduction is a good way to connect with people in your network whom you don't connect with directly. Although you can send an invitation to connect to someone you don't know, you might want to consider requesting an introduction through a shared connection for important communications. An introduction can carry more weight than a cold contact.

For example, let's say that you're connected to your former manager Felice (1st degree connection) and Felice is connected to Dalton (2nd degree connection), a manager at another local company. You're very interested in working in Dalton's department, but you don't know him and haven't seen any posted job openings. Rather than sending Dalton an email and resume as a cold contact, you could send an introduction request through Felice.

Often you'll know already how you're connected to the person you want to reach, but you can also determine this by viewing the How You're Connected To [First Name] section in the right column of your target contact's profile. If you don't already know of a common connection, this section could list a name you recognize.

Here are several tips for making the most of LinkedIn introductions:

▶ **Talk to your 1st degree connection before sending an introduction request on LinkedIn.** Your connection might have information that's pertinent to your request. For example, if you're trying to reach someone about job opportunities, your connection might know if your target is hiring or if there's a more suitable person to contact.

▶ **Focus on introductions to 2nd degree connections for best results.** Although you can request an introduction to a 3rd degree connection, this requires two intermediaries. In many cases, the second intermediary (your 2nd degree connection passing on your request to your 3rd degree connection) might not even know you.

▶ **Make your introduction request concise and specific.** A vague request to "get to know" someone isn't nearly as effective as stating your specific purpose, such as seeking employment, recruiting for a job, offering consulting services, and so forth.

▶ **Keep in mind that you can have only five open introductions at one time with a free LinkedIn basic account.** You can find out how many introductions you still have available on the

Account & Settings page (go to the global navigation bar, click the down arrow to the left of your name, and select Settings from the drop-down menu). To increase your number of open introductions, you need to upgrade to a premium account. LinkedIn recommends using introductions judiciously rather than as a tool to contact hundreds of members.

To request an introduction, follow these steps:

1. Click the Get Introduced Through a Connection link on the profile of the person you want to reach. The Introductions page opens, shown in Figure 6.7.

FIGURE 6.7   Requesting an introduction to someone your connection knows.

TIP: **Other Ways to Request an Introduction**

You can also request an introduction by clicking the Get Introduced link in search results or group member lists.

---

2. If you don't want to share your contact information with the person you want to reach, remove the check mark from the Include

My Contact Information check box (selected by default). In general, it's a good idea to share contact information. To do so, enter your email address and phone number in the specified fields.

3. From the Category drop-down list, select the reason for your introduction request. Options include career opportunity, consulting offer, new venture, job inquiry, expertise request, business deal, reference request, or get back in touch.

4. In the Subject field, enter the subject of your request.

5. In the first text box, enter your message to the person you want to be introduced to.

6. In the second text box, enter a brief note to the person you want to make the referral (your 1st degree connection).

7. Click the Send button to send your introduction request.

Your 1st degree connection receives your request and can choose to forward it to your target connection with comments or decline your request. If your request wasn't clear, your connection might ask you for more information.

See the following section, "Managing Introduction Requests," for more information about the next step in the process.

Managing Introduction Requests

In addition to requesting your own introductions to others, you might also receive introduction requests. For example, LinkedIn members might ask you to facilitate an introduction to one of your connections or might ask your connection to facilitate an introduction to you.

To review and respond to introduction requests, follow these steps:

1. On the global navigation bar, click the Inbox link to open your Inbox.

2. Click the All Messages link and select Introductions from the drop-down menu. Your Inbox displays only your introduction requests. Alternatively, you can also view new introduction

requests in your Inbox preview on your home page or receive
them by email. (Specify this on the Account & Settings page.)

3. To open the request, click the subject line link. Figure 6.8 illustrates a sample introduction request.

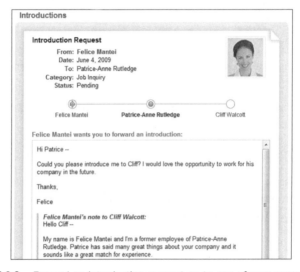

FIGURE 6.8   Forward an introduction request on to one of your connections.

4. Click the Forward button to forward the request to your connection.

> NOTE: **Declining an Introduction Request**
>
> If you don't want to make the introduction, click the Decline button,
> select a reason why you feel the introduction isn't a good fit, and
> click the Send button. The person who requested the introduction
> will receive your feedback on why you declined the introduction.

5. Enter any additional comments in the text box and click the
Forward Message button.

The target recipient receives your forwarded introduction request and can accept or decline it. Accepting the introduction enables the requestor and target to communicate with each other, but they still need to send an invitation request to become connections.

Summary

In this lesson, you learned about the many ways to communicate with other LinkedIn members and the options available based on their connection to you. Next, you learn how to search for people on LinkedIn.

LESSON 7
Searching on LinkedIn

In this lesson, you learn about LinkedIn quick searches, searching for people, advanced search techniques, and the Profile Organizer.

Performing a Quick Search

LinkedIn is a large, complex network of information. You can greatly improve your chances of achieving your networking goals by learning how to find exactly what you want among millions of member profiles and many more millions of answers, job postings, and group discussions. The easiest way to search for information on LinkedIn is to use the search box on LinkedIn's global navigation bar, shown in Figure 7.1.

FIGURE 7.1   Quickly search for information from anywhere on LinkedIn.

To perform a quick search, follow these steps:

1. Select the focus of your search from the drop-down list. Options include searching for people (the default), jobs, companies, answers, your Inbox, and groups.

2. Enter your search term in the text box. This might be a person's name, company name, job title, job skill, or a keyword, for example.

3. Click the Search button (a small white magnifying glass on a blue button). LinkedIn displays search results. The format of the search results depends on the type of search you perform.

This lesson focuses on LinkedIn's most popular search type (the people search) and advanced search techniques. To learn more about searching for jobs, companies, answers, your Inbox, and groups, refer to the lessons in this book that cover those topics.

Searching for People

The fastest way to search for people is to perform a quick search from the search box on LinkedIn's global navigation bar. For example, let's say that you're searching for your former colleague Felice Mantei. Enter her name in the search box and click the Search button. Your search results appear, shown in Figure 7.2.

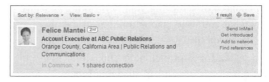

FIGURE 7.2   It's easy to find colleagues and classmates on LinkedIn.

NOTE: **LinkedIn Helps You Find Matches as You Type**

As you type, LinkedIn displays a drop-down list of potential matches in your network of connections. If you see a match in this list, click the member's name to open that member's profile.

Each LinkedIn member who matches your search results appears in a preview box that includes a photo, name, headline, location, industry, and information about shared connections and groups. Depending on the preview you're viewing, not all items might appear. For example, a member might choose not to upload a photo.

Icons appear to the right of each member's name indicating their connection to you, such as a 1st degree connection, 2nd degree connection, 3rd degree connection, or group member. For members who are out of your network, you might view the Out of Network designation next to their name or their name might be hidden from view.

Refer to Lesson 6, "Communicating with Other LinkedIn Members," for a reminder of how LinkedIn classifies its members.

Hover over the preview of a specific LinkedIn member to view the available contact links. (The preview box turns blue.) Possible links include Send Message, Get Introduced, Send InMail, Add to Network, Find References, or Save Profile. The options available depend on your connection to the particular member. For example, it wouldn't make sense for you to send InMail or get introduced to someone you already connect with. Refer to Lesson 6 for more information about the available options for contacting others on LinkedIn.

NOTE: **LinkedIn Limits the Number of Members You Can View**

With a personal account, you can view 100 results at a time. To view more results, you need to upgrade to a premium account. To learn more about premium accounts, click the Upgrade Your Account link on the bottom navigation menu.

Narrowing People Search Results

When you search for the name of a specific individual, the search results should display a short list (unless the individual has a very common name). But what if you can't remember someone's last name or you're searching for LinkedIn members who meet specific criteria such CPAs in the Indianapolis area? In this case, your search might return hundreds or even thousands of results, exceeding the 100-result viewing limits associated with a personal account.

There are two ways to handle this. One is to narrow the results that display on your search results page. The other is to perform an advanced search that targets very specific criteria.

On the search results page, you can sort the search results using the following criteria:

▶ **Relevance:** Displays search results in the order LinkedIn determines most appropriate based on keywords you enter and your network.

▶ **Relationship:** Displays search results based on their position in your network, in the following order: 1st degree connections,

2nd degree connections, fellow group members, and 3rd degree
connections that are combined with out-of-network connections.

- ▶ **Relationship + Recommendations:** Displays search results by
  relationship. Those that have the most recommendations are listed first for each relationship category.

- ▶ **Connections:** Displays search results based on the number of
  common connections.

- ▶ **Keyword:** Displays search results that match your keywords
  without considering their placement in your network.

You can also customize the member information you preview in your
search results. The options are

- ▶ **Basic:** Displays a photo, name, professional headline, location,
  industry, and details about shared connections.

- ▶ **Expanded:** Displays all the information from the basic view and
  current and past employment details.

- ▶ **Create a New View:** Opens the Create a New View pop-up box
  (see Figure 7.3) in which you can specify the exact information
  you want to display in the preview. Options include the data you
  can see in Basic and Expanded views and recommendations,
  groups, and number of connections. Click the Save button to save
  your customized view for future use. Customized views are a
  premium feature for customers who upgrade to a paid account.

FIGURE 7.3   Customize exactly what you see in search results.

The other way to narrow search results is to click the Show More link in the Search box to display more options for narrowing your search, as shown in Figure 7.4.

FIGURE 7.4   Modify your search criteria to narrow your results.

In this box, you can narrow your search results by specifying any of the following criteria:

▶ **Keywords:** Enter a keyword that LinkedIn searches for in member profiles. The best keywords are terms that don't fit any of the other search criteria and are specific words that a member might include on a profile. For example, entering a name or location wouldn't be appropriate here, but terms such as *Java*, *PMP*, *auditing*, *CPA*, and so forth would work well.

▶ **First Name:** Enter the first name of the member you want to find.

▶ **Last Name:** Enter the last name of the member you want to find.

▶ **Title:** Enter a job title and specify in the drop-down list whether you want to search only for members who hold this title currently, in the past, or both currently and in the past.

▶ **Company:** Enter a company name and specify in the drop-down list whether you want to search only for members who work at this company currently, in the past, or both currently and in the past.

▶ **School:** Enter the name of a college or university.

▶ **Location:** Select a country, postal code, and distance range.

▶ **Keep Filter Selections:** Select this check box to save your choices in the search box.

Click the Search button to update the search results.

For even more search options, consider the choices in the Filter By box (below the Search box): Location, Relationship, Industry, Current Company, Past Company, School, or Profile Language. If you have a premium account, LinkedIn offers even more advanced search options such as Groups, Company Size, and Seniority Level. Again, click the Search button to update results.

Performing an Advanced People Search

If you want to search for very specific criteria, you can perform an advanced people search. An advanced search offers you the same options as the extended version of the Search box on the search results page, but you can perform it all in one step. For example, you might enter a search term in the quick search box and then decide to narrow your results. But if you already know that you want to search for specific keywords, companies, or locations, for example, an advanced search is a more streamlined option.

To perform an advanced people search, select the People option (if it's not already selected by default) to the left of the search box that appears on the global navigation bar and click the Advanced link. Figure 7.5 shows the Advanced People Search page.

FIGURE 7.5 LinkedIn's advanced people search options provide maximum flexibility in finding members who meet specific criteria.

Enter your search criteria on this page and click the Search button to display your search results. Refer to "Narrowing People Search Results," earlier in this lesson for descriptions of each field on this page.

> NOTE: **Performing a Reference Search**
>
> From the Advanced People Search page, you can click the Reference Search tab to search for potential references for a job candidate. See Web Lesson 1, "Recruiting Job Candidates," for more information about reference searches.

Saving a People Search

If you perform the same searches frequently, saving them can reduce redundant data entry. To save a search for future use, follow these steps:

1. Click the Save link on the search results page.

2. In the Save This People Search pop-up box, enter a search name for this search (see Figure 7.6).

FIGURE 7.6   Saving a search saves you time.

3. In the Send Email Alert field, choose to receive email updates of your search results: Weekly, Monthly, or Never. You don't have to receive updates by email, but this can be a time-saver if you're very interested in following updates to your saved search. For example, recruiters might want to know about new LinkedIn members who match specific search criteria. Or job seekers might want to know about new LinkedIn members who work at companies they're interested in working for.

NOTE: **LinkedIn Limits the Number of Searches You Can Save**

As a free basic account holder, you can save up to three searches and receive email updates either weekly or monthly. To save more searches, click the Upgrade Your Account link to sign up for a premium account. If you want to receive daily email updates on your saved searches, you must select the Pro account option.

---

4. Click the Save button to save your search.

5. Click the Close This Window link to close the confirmation pop-up box.

To edit or delete your saved searches, click the Saved Searches tab on the search results page.

Using Advanced Search Techniques

LinkedIn offers several techniques for narrowing your search results even further. You can use these techniques when performing a quick search or when using the Advanced People Search page. For example, you can search for phrases in quotation marks, use search operators such as NOT and OR, or enter complex criteria with a parenthetical search.

LinkedIn enables you to use specific search operators to define advanced criteria directly in the quick search box. For example, *ccompany* is the operator for current company and *title* is the operator for job title. Entering **ccompany:Google title:director** would quickly list all current Google employees with the title of director.

For more information about advanced search techniques, visit the LinkedIn Learning Center at http://learn.linkedin.com/linkedin-search. Scroll down the page to the "Advanced Search Tips" section.

Using the Profile Organizer

LinkedIn's Profile Organizer enables you to save profiles of interest, sort them into folders, and add notes about your contact with the members whose profiles you save. This feature is particularly useful for recruiters, active job seekers, or people using LinkedIn for business development. You must have a premium LinkedIn account (this includes Job Seeker accounts) or sign up for a free Profile Organizer trial to use this useful tool. Depending on the plan you choose, you can maintain from 5 to 75 Profile Organizer folders.

Figure 7.7 shows a sample Profile Organizer view.

In the Profile Organizer, you can do the following:

► **Add and view notes about each person whose profile you saved:** Notes can contain up to 1,000 characters. This is a good place to flag profiles for follow-up, indicate where you met a particular contact, and so forth.

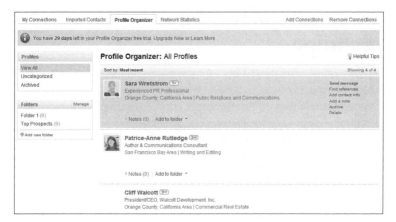

FIGURE 7.7 Save and manage LinkedIn member profiles with the Profile Organizer.

▶ **Add profiles to folders:** For example, you might want to create folders for potential recruitment prospects, potential clients, people you met at a conference, hiring managers at companies you want to work for, and so forth.

▶ **Contact a LinkedIn member whose profile you saved:** To view potential options, pause your mouse over the profile and view the contact options on the right side of the profile preview box. Depending on your connection to the person and what actions you've already taken, possible options include the following links: Send Message, Send InMail, Add Contact Info, Contact Information, Add a Note, Archive, and Delete.

To access Profile Organizer, select Profile Organizer from the Contacts drop-down menu on the global navigation bar. Click the Upgrade Now button to upgrade to a paid account immediately or click the Start a 30-Day Free Trial link to receive a 30-day free trial of the Profile Organizer. No credit card is required for the free trial.

> **NOTE: Consider Free Alternatives to the Profile Organizer**
> Free alternatives to the Profile Organizer include the Bookmark Profile features available with the LinkedIn Firefox browser toolbar and the LinkedIn Internet Explorer toolbar. Although bookmarking profiles in your browser doesn't offer the advanced features and flexibility of the Profile Organizer, it is a viable alternative for those on a tight budget.

Summary

In this lesson, you learned how to find information quickly and easily through LinkedIn's advanced search capabilities. Next, you learn about several tools that also enhance searching and other aspects of your LinkedIn experience.

LESSON 8

Using LinkedIn Tools

In this lesson, you learn about the tools that enable you to access LinkedIn data from other websites and software.

Understanding LinkedIn Tools

LinkedIn offers several tools, toolbars, and widgets that enhance your LinkedIn experience, both on and off the site. Options include

- ▶ **Browser Toolbar:** Search and access LinkedIn data from Firefox or Internet Explorer.

- ▶ **JobsInsider:** Discover members of your LinkedIn network who work at companies whose job postings you're viewing. JobsInsider is included with the Browser Toolbar.

- ▶ **Outlook Toolbar:** Manage your LinkedIn network from Microsoft Outlook.

- ▶ **Email Signature:** Create a customized email signature from your profile data to use with popular email systems.

- ▶ **Google Toolbar Assistant:** Add a LinkedIn search button to the Google Toolbar.

- ▶ **Mac Search Widget:** Search LinkedIn from your Mac Dashboard.

- ▶ **Mobile:** Access your LinkedIn network via mobile devices, such as the iPhone, BlackBerry, and Palm Pre.

- ▶ **LinkedIn Widget for Lotus Notes:** Integrate your LinkedIn content with Lotus Notes. You can access LinkedIn tools from the Tools link on the bottom navigation menu.

Installing and Using the LinkedIn Firefox Browser Toolbar

The LinkedIn Firefox Browser Toolbar, also called the LinkedIn Companion for Firefox, is available for a PC or Mac running Firefox versions 2.0 or 3.0. System requirements include Windows XP/Vista or Mac OS X 10.2 or later.

TIP: **Mac Users Should Also Consider the Mac Search Widget**

Another option for Mac users is the Mac Search Widget, which enables you to search LinkedIn from your Mac Dashboard. The widget requires OS 10.4. To download the widget, click the Tools link on LinkedIn's bottom navigation menu, and then click the Download It Now button in the Mac Search Widget section.

To install the LinkedIn Firefox Browser Toolbar, follow these steps:

1. Click the Tools link on the bottom navigation menu.

2. In the Browser Toolbar box, pause your mouse over the Download It Now button and select Firefox (Macintosh and PC) from the drop-down menu.

3. Click the Install Now button in the window that appears. Depending on your operating system, you might have to allow Firefox to install this application.

4. Restart Firefox to complete your changes.

Firefox displays a welcome screen and the toolbar now appears on the menu (see Figure 8.1).

If the LinkedIn button doesn't appear on your browser toolbar, try one of the following:

▶ Verify that you meet all the listed system requirements.

▶ Click the View menu, click Toolbars, and then click LinkedIn to display the LinkedIn toolbar on Firefox.

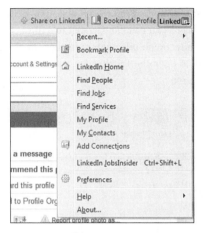

FIGURE 8.1   Use the LinkedIn Firefox Browser toolbar to locate information on LinkedIn.

▶ Click the View menu, click Toolbars, and then click Customize. In the Customize Toolbars dialog box, select Icons and Text from the Show drop-down list, drag the LinkedIn Companion icon to the toolbar, and click the Done button.

Click the LinkedIn button on your browser toolbar to display a drop-down list of options. These include

▶ **Recent:** Displays links to your recent profile, recent searches, and job page views. To clear this data, click the Remove options.

▶ **Bookmark LinkedIn Page:** Lets you create a Firefox bookmark for an active LinkedIn page. This option is available only if you're viewing a LinkedIn page that you can bookmark, such as a profile, search results, or a job listing.

▶ **LinkedIn Home:** Takes you to LinkedIn's home page. This section also includes direct links to Find People, Find Jobs, Find Services, My Profile, My Contacts, and Add Connections.

▶ **LinkedIn JobsInsider:** Opens the LinkedIn JobsInsider window. See the "Using the JobsInsider" section later in this lesson for more information.

▶ **Preferences:** Opens the Preferences dialog box, shown in
Figure 8.2, where you can enter your LinkedIn account information, specify how much information to show on the Recent menu,
specify when to open the JobsInsider, and activate the InfoBox in
Web email option.

FIGURE 8.2   Specify what you want to display on the Appearance menu of
the toolbar.

▶ **Help:** Opens a help file in which you can search for more information.

▶ **About:** Displays information about the toolbar.

The toolbar also includes the Share on LinkedIn button, which enables you
to share web pages in a LinkedIn update. See "Sharing Web Pages with
LinkedIn Members" later in this lesson for more information.

To uninstall the toolbar, select Tools, Add-Ons from the Firefox menu and
click the Uninstall button in the LinkedIn Companion for Firefox section.

Installing and Using the LinkedIn Internet Explorer Toolbar

The LinkedIn Internet Explorer Toolbar is available for the PC only.
Although LinkedIn lists official support for Microsoft Windows 2000/XP,
with Microsoft Internet Explorer 6.0 and 7.0, you should be able to install
this app on Windows Vista and Windows 7 as well.

To install the LinkedIn Internet Explorer Toolbar, follow these steps:

1. Click the Tools link on the bottom navigation menu.

2. In the Browser Toolbar box, pause your mouse over the Download It Now button and select Internet Explorer (PC Only) from the drop-down menu.

3. Click the Run button. The LinkedIn Internet Explorer Toolbar Setup dialog box appears, shown in Figure 8.3.

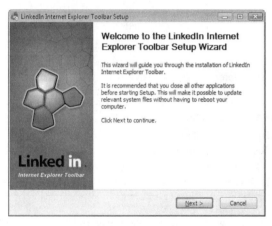

FIGURE 8.3   Setting up the LinkedIn Internet Explorer Toolbar.

4. Click the Next button to continue.

5. Select the check box to accept the license agreement and click the Next button.

6. Accept the default installation folder and click the Install button. Alternatively, click the Browse button to select another folder.

7. A warning dialog box prompts you to close all open Internet Explorer windows. Do so, and click the Yes button to continue.

8. Select the Launch Internet Explorer with LinkedIn Toolbar check box and click the Finish button.

Internet Explorer opens with the toolbar installed, shown in Figure 8.4.

FIGURE 8.4   Search, access, and bookmark pages from LinkedIn while using Internet Explorer.

NOTE: Where Is the LinkedIn Toolbar?

If the LinkedIn toolbar doesn't appear, select View, Toolbars, LinkedIn Toolbar from the browser menu (the exact menu location varies by operating system). Also verify that you meet the system requirements to install the toolbar.

Click the down arrow to the right of the LinkedIn button on your browser toolbar to display a drop-down list of options. These include

▶ **LinkedIn Home:** Takes you to LinkedIn's home page. This section also includes direct links to Find People, Find Jobs, Find Services, My Profile, and My Contacts.

▶ **Preferences:** Opens the Preferences dialog box, in which you can enter your LinkedIn account information, specify when to open the JobsInsider, and activate the InfoBox in Web email option.

▶ **Help:** Opens a help file where you can search for more information.

▶ **Check for Update:** Checks to see whether there is a more recent version of the toolbar.

▶ **About:** Displays information about the toolbar.

The LinkedIn Toolbar also includes the following buttons:

▶ **Search:** Click the down arrow to the right of the search button to select search options. Options include all keywords, name, title, current title, company, current company, and jobs. Enter your search term, and click the Search button to display relevant results in LinkedIn. You can also select the Clear Search History menu to clear your searches or the Advanced Search option to open the Advanced Search page in LinkedIn.

▶ **Bookmarks:** Click the Bookmark This page menu option to bookmark an active LinkedIn page. This option is available only if you're viewing a LinkedIn page that you can bookmark, such as a profile, search results, or a job listing. Select the Manage Bookmarks to open the Bookmarks window.

▶ **JobsInsider:** Opens the JobsInsider window. See the "Using the JobsInsider" section later in this lesson for more information.

▶ **Share in LinkedIn:** Enables you to share web pages in a LinkedIn update. See "Sharing Web Pages with LinkedIn Members" later in this lesson for more information.

To remove the LinkedIn Internet Explorer Toolbar, go to the Control Panel and delete it. The exact path to access the Control Panel varies by operating system.

Using JobsInsider

LinkedIn JobsInsider is a LinkedIn Browser Toolbar feature that assists in your job search. When you're viewing a job posting, JobsInsider lets you know about LinkedIn members in your network who work at that company and are potential inside connections for you. JobsInsider works with job postings on sites such as Monster, CareerBuilder, HotJobs, Craigslist, Simply Hired, Dice, or Vault.

NOTE: **You Must Install the LinkedIn Browser Toolbar to Use JobsInsider**

If you haven't installed the LinkedIn Browser Toolbar yet, click the JobsInsider link on the bottom navigation menu for installation instructions. See the "Installing and Using the LinkedIn Firefox Browser Toolbar" section and the "Installing and Using the LinkedIn Internet Explorer Toolbar" section earlier in this lesson for more information.

For example, if you're searching Monster.com for potential jobs, JobsInsider opens automatically, detecting that you're searching a job site. Figure 8.5 shows a sample view of JobsInsider.

FIGURE 8.5   JobsInsider points out your inside connections at a hiring company.

When you open a job posting, JobsInsider lists the names of your 1st degree connections and includes links to their LinkedIn profiles. It also tells you the total people in your network who work at this company. Click the number to view a list of these people.

NOTE: **You Can Activate and Deactivate JobsInsider**

To specify JobsInsider settings, click the LinkedIn button on your browser toolbar and select Preferences from the menu. In the Preferences dialog box, you can specify whether you want to open JobsInsider when browsing a known job site, open at browser start-up, or not open at all.

Sharing Web Pages with LinkedIn Members

If you've installed the LinkedIn Browser Toolbar for either Firefox or Internet Explorer, you can easily share news stories, blog posts, and other interesting web content with LinkedIn members, including your connections and fellow members of groups.

To share web pages, follow these steps:

1. In your browser, navigate to the page you want to share.

2. Click the Share on LinkedIn button (Firefox) or Share in LinkedIn button (Internet Explorer) on the toolbar.

   If you can't find these buttons, click the Tools link on the bottom navigation menu and then click the Sharing Bookmarklet tab to install this manually.

3. The pop-up box that opens (see Figure 8.6) displays fields that are nearly identical to what you see when you post an update. (Refer to Lesson 5, "Managing and Updating Your Profile," for more information.) Make any modifications, enter your own comments, and click the Share button to share this web page.

FIGURE 8.6 Share selected web pages with LinkedIn connections or group members.

The content you share displays at the top of your profile and in the Network Activity section of your connections' home pages, just like a regular update.

Although this feature provides a convenient way to share content on LinkedIn, it's a powerful tool that you shouldn't overuse. To generate a positive response from other LinkedIn members, focus on sharing only the most useful, relevant content that affects the majority of group members. For example, share a top news story or an insightful report that affects your industry. Don't share promotional material, sales pages, or your daily blog posts (unless one contains highly useful or relevant content).

Using the Outlook Toolbar

With the Outlook Toolbar, you can manage your LinkedIn network from within Microsoft Outlook. The toolbar requires that you run Windows XP or Vista and use Microsoft Outlook XP (2002), 2003, or 2007.

> TIP: **Check Out the LinkedIn Outlook Connector**
> Also consider the LinkedIn Outlook Connector (http://www.linkedin.com/outlook), which requires the latest version of Outlook Social Connector (download it from Microsoft) and Outlook 2003, 2007, or 2010, which integrates Outlook and LinkedIn.

To install the Outlook Toolbar, close Outlook and follow these steps:

1. Click the Tools link on the bottom navigation menu.

2. In the Outlook Toolbar box, click the Download It Now button.

3. Click the OK button to confirm that you are located in one of the countries listed in the pop-up box.

4. Click Run to run the file. The LinkedIn Outlook Toolbar Setup dialog box opens.

5. Click the Next button to continue.

6. Select the check box to accept the license agreement and click the Next button.

7. Accept the default installation folder and click the Install button. Alternatively, click the Browse button to select another folder.

8. Select the Launch Microsoft Outlook with LinkedIn Outlook Toolbar check box and click the Finish button.

The LinkedIn toolbar and menu now appear in Outlook. The toolbar enables you to

▶ Receive suggestions about who to connect with on LinkedIn based on email frequency

▶ Send LinkedIn invitations with one click

▶ Update Outlook based on LinkedIn profile data

▶ Get notified when your contacts update their LinkedIn profiles

▶ Stay current with your network using the LinkedIn dashboard

▶ Search and access LinkedIn data from Outlook

NOTE: **Troubleshooting the Outlook Toolbar**

The installation of the Outlook Toolbar might require different steps based on your browser, operating system, and configuration. Refer to LinkedIn's online help for the latest news on toolbar updates and changes.

Creating an Email Signature

LinkedIn enables you to create an email signature that includes links to your profile and other popular LinkedIn features. You can use your LinkedIn email signature with popular email systems such as Microsoft Outlook, Outlook Express, Mozilla Thunderbird, and Yahoo! Mail.

To create an email signature, follow these steps:

1. Click the Tools link on the bottom navigation menu.

2. In the Email Signature section of the LinkedIn Tools page, click the Try It Now button. The Create Email Signature page opens, shown in Figure 8.7.

FIGURE 8.7   Create an email signature you can use with many popular email systems.

3. Select a layout for your email signature from the drop-down list. A preview of your signature with the selected layout appears on the page. To view all the options at once, click the View Gallery link.

4. Enter the contact information you want to appear on your signature in the Business Information, Contact Information, and Work Address sections.

5. If you want to include a company logo or your photo, enter the image's URL in the Image Selection field. Your image must be in

the GIF, JPG, or PNG format; no larger than 50KB; and no larger than 100 × 60 in size. Click the Show link to display your image. Be aware that the way you add an image could vary depending on the browser you're using.

NOTE: **You Can Use Your LinkedIn Profile Photo on Your Signature**

To use your LinkedIn photo, right-click the photo on your profile and choose Copy Image Location or Copy Shortcut from the menu. (The menu option varies by browser.) Paste (Ctrl+V) this link in the Image Selection field.

---

6. Select any or all of the following check boxes to place links on your email signature: Professional Profile link, See Who We Know in Common link, or We're Hiring link.

7. Click the Click Here for Instructions link to save your signature. A new window opens, shown in Figure 8.8.

8. Copy your signature code by clicking in the text box and pressing Ctrl+C on your keyboard.

9. Select your email client from the drop-down list. Instructions for using the email signature in your email system appear.

10. Click the Close This Window link (at the bottom of the window) to close the window and install your new email signature.

Using the Google Toolbar Assistant

The Google Toolbar Assistant optimizes the Google Toolbar by installing a LinkedIn search button. You need to the Google Toolbar (http://toolbar.google.com) for Firefox or Internet Explorer to use this feature.

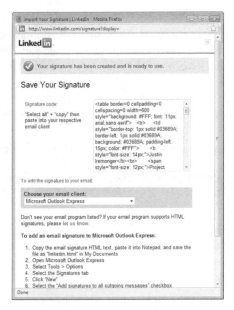

FIGURE 8.8   Copy and paste the code for your new email signature into your email system.

To install the Google Toolbar Assistant, follow these steps:

1. Click the Tools link on the bottom navigation menu.

2. In the Google Toolbar Assistant section of the LinkedIn Tools page, click the Download It Now button. The Google Toolbar Custom Button Installer dialog box opens. If you haven't installed the Google Toolbar yet, you're prompted to do so before continuing.

3. Click the Add button.

4. In the dialog box that opens, specify whether you want to search by keywords or name in the Search Method field. You can change this later (see Figure 8.9).

5. Click the OK button. LinkedIn places the LinkedIn search button on the Google Toolbar (see Figure 8.10).

FIGURE 8.9   Add a LinkedIn button on the Google Toolbar.

FIGURE 8.10   Quickly search for information on LinkedIn.

To use the search button, enter a search term in the text box and click the LinkedIn button. LinkedIn displays results based on the type of search method you specified (either a keyword or a name).

To change your search method or remove the search button, right-click the LinkedIn button.

Summary

In this lesson, you learned how to install and use tools that help you integrate LinkedIn with other popular websites and software programs.

LESSON 9

Finding a Job

In this lesson, you learn how to use LinkedIn as an effective job search tool, find and apply to job postings, and use LinkedIn's many other features for job seekers.

Attracting Recruiters and Hiring Managers

LinkedIn is an excellent tool for job seekers, but you need to create a stellar profile and develop a solid network if you want to maximize your results. Here are seven tips for making the most of LinkedIn as a job search tool.

1. **Complete your profile:** LinkedIn reports that members with a complete profile generate 40 times more opportunities than those whose profiles aren't complete.

2. **Develop a solid network of connections:** Your ability to use job search features such as JobsInsider or Inside Connections depends on having a reasonable number of connections. You should aim for at least 50 connections to maximize the benefits of these features, although they do work with fewer connections.

3. **Get recommendations:** A complete profile includes at least three recommendations. Aim for recommendations from managers, executives, or actual clients. Peer recommendations, particularly those that you "trade" with colleagues by recommending each other, carry far less weight.

4. **Include keywords that are relevant to your profession and industry:** These include specific skills, certifications, and

degrees. Recruiters search for these words, and your profile should include them if you want to be found.

5. **Focus on results, not a list of duties:** Remember that your profile is a concise summary of your qualifications, not a resume. (Although you can attach one if you like.) Emphasize your results and accomplishments; don't just list tasks you performed.

6. **Post a resume or portfolio:** Using LinkedIn applications such as Box.net Files, you can attach PDFs to your profile.

7. **Indicate on your profile that you're seeking employment:** If you're unemployed, include this information in your status, professional headline, or summary. Don't sound desperate, but do let your network know that you're looking for opportunities.

See Lesson 2, "Creating Your Profile," and Lesson 10, "Requesting and Providing Recommendations," for more information.

TIP: **Clean Up Your Digital Dirt Before Your Job Search**

Keep in mind that many recruiters now search the web for background information on potential candidates. It isn't enough to have a professional presence on LinkedIn. Review any other social networking profiles you have to ensure they also reinforce your professional image. If not, remove your "digital dirt" before you begin your job search. Also, verify that your contacts don't post photos or other content about you that would compromise your professional reputation.

Searching Job Postings

LinkedIn offers a large database of job postings that are posted directly on LinkedIn and on its partner site, Simply Hired.

TIP: **LinkedIn Offers Other Ways to Find Job Postings**

Although the Jobs page is LinkedIn's primary job search tool, you should also search the Jobs Discussion Board for any group you belong to and the Careers tab on the company profiles for your tar-

get employers. To do a quick search for jobs, use the search box
on the top navigation menu.

To search job postings on LinkedIn, follow these steps:

1. On the global navigation bar, click the Jobs link. The Jobs page
opens, shown in Figure 9.1.

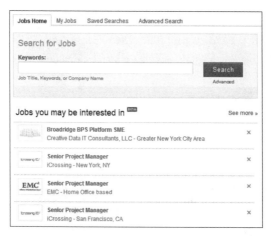

FIGURE 9.1   On the Jobs page, you can review suggested jobs based on
your profile or search for jobs by keyword.

NOTE: **View Jobs LinkedIn Recommends for You**

Below the search box on the Jobs page, LinkedIn lists jobs you
might be interested in based on the information you entered on
your profile. For example, if you work in project management, you
could view a list of jobs in this field.

2. In the Search for Jobs box, enter keywords related to your job
search. For example, you could enter a job title, a job skill, or the
name of a target company.

3. Click the Search button. The Job Search Results page opens,
shown in Figure 9.2.

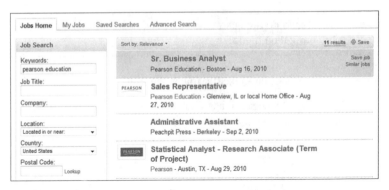

FIGURE 9.2   Viewing a list of jobs that match your criteria.

On this page, you can do the following:

▶ Sort jobs by relevance, your relationship to the job poster, or the date posted (most recent or earliest).

▶ Identify the company by its logo (not available for all postings).

▶ Open the job posting by clicking the job title link.

▶ Save this job search and have results sent to you via email on a regular basis, such as daily, weekly, or monthly.

▶ Save a specific job posting by pausing the mouse over it and clicking the Save Job link. You can review the jobs you save at a later time by clicking the My Jobs link on the Jobs page.

▶ View jobs similar to a specific job posting by pausing the mouse over it and clicking the Similar Jobs link. LinkedIn displays jobs that are the most similar to the one you selected.

▶ Refine your search criteria using the fields on the left side of the page. The fields in the Job Search box are nearly identical to the fields on the Advanced Search page. See "Performing an Advanced Job Search" later in this chapter for more information.

Viewing Job Postings

The content listed on a job posting varies according to what the hiring company chooses to display. The content that you see will also vary according to what type of connection you have to the poster and the connections you have to the people working at that company. A job posting (see Figure 9.3) might include some or all of the following features:

▶ A header listing the job title, location, and company URL.

▶ A detailed job description.

▶ The Apply Now button. Click this button to apply for the job from LinkedIn. See the "Applying for a Job" section later in this lesson for more information. Alternatively, the Apply on Company Website button might display if a company prefers to use its own application process.

▶ The Request Introduction button. Click this button to open the Introductions page where you can request an introduction to the job poster. You can request introductions only to job posters in your network. Otherwise, the Request Introduction button doesn't appear. Refer to Lesson 6, "Communicating with Other LinkedIn Members," for more information about LinkedIn introductions.

▶ The Save Job link. Click to save this job for future viewing on the My Jobs page.

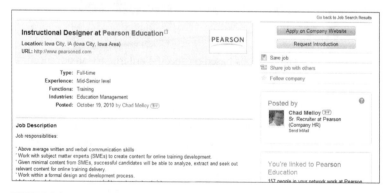

FIGURE 9.3 Viewing a list of jobs that match specified criteria.

▸ The Share Job with Others link. Click to send a message to a connection who might be interested in this job.

▸ The Follow Company link, which enables you to follow this company's activity on LinkedIn.

▸ The Bookmark link, which enables you to bookmark this job on Internet Explorer. You won't see this option if you aren't using Internet Explorer as your browser.

▸ The Posted By box with a link to the job poster's LinkedIn profile. A connection icon appears if this person is in your network. For example, if a job poster is connected to one of your connections, the 2nd degree connection icon appears.

▸ The You're Linked to [Company Name] box. Click one of the links in this box to display the LinkedIn members in your network who work at this company. These people could provide you inside information about potential job opportunities at the company. If you aren't linked to anyone at this company, the You Aren't Linked to [Company Name] box opens, which encourages you to expand your network.

▸ The Similar Jobs box, which lists jobs that are similar to the one you're viewing.

Performing an Advanced Job Search

If you want to search for jobs based on specific criteria, try an advanced job search:

1. On the global navigation bar, click the Jobs link.

2. Click the Advanced Search tab on the Jobs page. You can also open this page by clicking the Advanced link when searching for jobs from the search box on the global navigation bar. Figure 9.4 shows the Advanced Search page.

3. In the Keywords text box, enter keywords (such as a job title, a skill, or a certification). Refer to Lesson 7, "Searching on LinkedIn," for more information on using advanced search criteria.

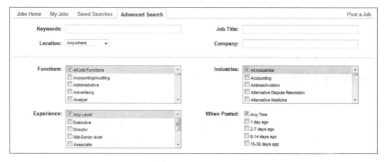

FIGURE 9.4   Performing an advanced job search.

4. Specify the criteria for your search. Options include the following:

▶ Location

▶ Job Title

▶ Company

▶ Functions (such as Accounting/Auditing, Engineering, Finance, Information Technology, Marketing, and so forth)

▶ Industries (such as Banking, Biotechnology, Computer Software, Insurance, Real Estate, and so forth)

▶ Experience (ranging from executive-level jobs to internships)

▶ When Posted (the date the job was posted, such as in the last day or at any time)

▶ Sort By (specific criteria such as date posted or relevance to your keywords)

5. Click the Search button to display job search results.

Refer to the earlier section, "Searching Job Postings," for more information about the job search results page.

> TIP: **Specify Only the Most Important Criteria**
> You don't need to specify criteria in all the fields available on the Advanced Search page. Start with a few choices and then narrow or expand your search based on your search results.

Applying for a Job

LinkedIn offers two ways to apply for jobs, based on the way the company posting a job handles its recruitment. If the Apply on Company Website button displays on a job posting, clicking this button takes you to the company's external website where you can apply for the job. If the Apply Now button displays on the job posting, clicking this button directs you to a job application form on LinkedIn. In this section, you learn how to complete LinkedIn's own job application form.

To apply for a job from a LinkedIn posting, following these steps:

1. In the job description for the job you would like to apply for, click the Apply Now button and an application page will display. Figure 9.5 shows a sample application page.

2. In the Contact Information section, enter details about your name, email address, and contact information.

3. In the Cover Letter and Resume section, enter your cover letter. A good cover letter summarizes strengths and accomplishments that are relevant to this job and is personalized for this target job.

4. Click the Browse button next to the Resume field to upload your resume as a text file, Word document, PDF, or HTML file of no more than 200KB. LinkedIn attaches your uploaded resume in its original format.

Step 1 - Apply for job

Contact Information

* Email Address: patrice@patricerutledge.com ▾
Add email addresses to your account

* Telephone Number:

* City:

State/Province:

* Country: United States   ▾

Best way to reach me:

Cover Letter and Resume

* Cover Letter:

FIGURE 9.5   Applying for jobs directly from LinkedIn.

5. Click the Continue button.

6. Review and confirm your application one more time before submitting. Be sure to check for spelling, grammar, and content.

7. Click the Apply Now button to submit your application for the job.

Finding Recruiters and Hiring Managers

The good news for job seekers: Thousands of recruiters and hiring managers maintain profiles on LinkedIn. To find them, select People in the quick search box on the global navigation bar. Then click the Advanced link to the right of the box to open the Advanced People Search page.

There are several ways to find recruiters and hiring managers on the Advanced Search page. Some examples include the following:

▶ In the Industries field, select Staffing and Recruiting and enter keywords related to the type of job you're looking for. If applicable, enter location criteria.

> ▶ Enter Recruiter in the Title field and the name of a company you want to work for.

> ▶ Enter Recruiter in the Title field plus relevant location information.

> ▶ Enter the name of a company you want to work for and select Hiring Managers from the Interested In drop-down list (if you have a premium account).

Searching for appropriate contacts is a combination of art and science, so you might need to revise your search criteria several times before you find the appropriate people.

CAUTION: **Don't Spam Recruiters and Hiring Managers**
Remember that LinkedIn is a networking and research tool, not a means of spamming prospective recruiters and employers. When you do find good targets for your job search, review their profiles carefully to determine the best way to contact them. Some recruiters provide links to external sites for job candidates. If your target is a hiring manager, determine whether you can reach this person through a network introduction. Alternatively, consider sending a brief message to hiring managers who indicate they are open to job inquiries.

Upgrading to a Job Seeker Premium Account

LinkedIn offers many free features and opportunities for job seekers. If you need access to LinkedIn premium features to aid in your job search, however, consider upgrading to a Job Seeker premium account. For example, these accounts can provide access to InMail, the Profile Organizer, and the OpenLink Network and increase your available introductions.

All Job Seeker premium accounts enable you to display a Job Seeker badge on your profile, receive placement as a featured applicant when you apply for a job, use premium search features, view who is interested in your profile, participate in the OpenLink Network (described in Lesson 1,

"Introducing LinkedIn"), and receive priority customer service from LinkedIn.

Table 9.1 shows the specific features for each level of Job Seeker account.

TABLE 9.1 Job Seeker Account Comparison

Feature	Basic	Job Seeker	Job Seeker Plus
Monthly Price	$19.95	$29.95	$49.95
InMails	None	5	10
Profile Organizer Folders	5	10	25
Profile Results per Search	100	250	500
Pending Introductions	10	15	25

To upgrade to a Job Seeker premium account or learn more about upgrade options, select Job Seeker Premium from the Jobs drop-down menu on the global navigation bar.

Summary

In this lesson, you learned about LinkedIn's many job search tools. In addition, you learned the most effective way to conduct a job search on LinkedIn.

LESSON 10

Requesting and Providing Recommendations

In this lesson, you learn how to request, provide, manage, and revise professional recommendations on LinkedIn.

Understanding LinkedIn Recommendations

LinkedIn enables you to request recommendations from and provide recommendations to the people in your professional network. Recommendations are a powerful networking tool, so consider carefully whom you want to ask for a recommendation and whom you want to recommend as part of your overall LinkedIn strategy.

LinkedIn offers four types of recommendations:

- ▶ **Colleague:** You worked with this person at the same company as a manager, peer, or employee.

- ▶ **Business Partner:** You worked with this person in another capacity, not as a colleague or client. For example, you worked at partner companies, performed volunteer or association work together, and so forth.

- ▶ **Student:** You were a teacher, advisor, or fellow student at the same school.

▶ **Service Provider:** You hired this person to perform services. Service Provider recommendations differ from the other recommendation types in that they also appear in the LinkedIn Service Providers directory. See Lesson 14, "Using LinkedIn Service Providers," for more information about service provider recommendations.

The recommendation process involves several steps between two people to ensure that both approve the recommendation before it is final. For example, if Anne wants to request a recommendation from her former manager, Sophie—a common type of request—the process requires four steps:

▶ **Step 1:** Anne sends a recommendation request to Sophie.

▶ **Step 2:** Sophie receives the request and submits a recommendation for Anne.

▶ **Step 3:** Anne receives a notification about Sophie's recommendation and accepts the recommendation.

▶ **Step 4:** LinkedIn displays the recommendation on Anne's profile.

Obviously, this process assumes that both Anne and Sophie approve each step. LinkedIn also offers options for you to request clarifications and changes. If you write an unsolicited recommendation for a connection without receiving a recommendation request, your process starts at step 2 with submitting the recommendation.

Requesting Recommendations

Receiving recommendations from managers, colleagues, and clients can help you achieve your networking goals on LinkedIn. LinkedIn suggests that a complete profile should include at least three recommendations for maximum effectiveness.

Before you send your requests, however, think about what you want to achieve. Be clear about your goals so that your connections write recommendations that help you achieve them. For example, if you want to move into a management position, you should request a recommendation that discusses your leadership abilities. If you want to change careers, emphasize crossover skills.

> TIP: **Let Your Connections Know You Want a Recommendation**
> Although LinkedIn notifies your connections that you've requested a recommendation, it's a good idea that this message doesn't come as a surprise. Talk to the people you want to recommend you so that they're aware of your request and know what to emphasize in their recommendation.

To request a recommendation from one of your connections, follow these steps:

1. On the global navigation bar, select Recommendations from the Profile drop-down menu. The Received Recommendations page opens, shown in Figure 10.1.

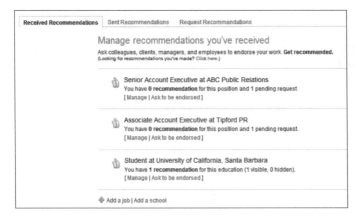

FIGURE 10.1   Ask your connections for professional recommendations to enhance your profile.

2. Click the Ask to Be Endorsed link next to the related position or school. The Request Recommendations page opens, shown in Figure 10.2.

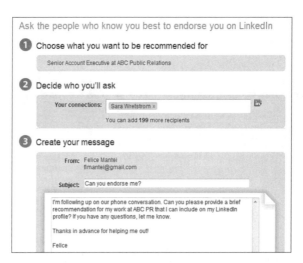

FIGURE 10.2   Requesting a recommendation is a simple process.

TIP: **Keep Your Profile Up to Date**

The Received Recommendations page displays only positions and schools you've already entered on your profile. If you haven't done this, click the Add a Job or Add a School link to complete this step first.

NOTE: **Request a Recommendation from Your Profile**

You can also request a recommendation on the Edit Profile page. To do so, click the Ask for a Recommendation link below the related position or school in the Experience or Education section. If you already have at least one recommendation, this link is called the Manage link.

3. In step 1, the position or school you selected appears by default. To change this, return to the previous page.

4. In step 2, start typing the name of the connection you want to ask for a recommendation. Select the correct name from the drop-down list of options that appear.

> **CAUTION: Don't Mass Produce Recommendation Requests**
> Although you can request a recommendation from up to 200 connections at a time, it's a much better practice to personalize each recommendation request you send. If you really want to send your request to more than one person, however, click the View All Connections button to select your recipients.

5. In step 3, create your message asking for a recommendation. LinkedIn provides sample text for you, but you should customize this for each request. Be specific and let your connection know what you want to achieve with this recommendation. You don't need to add a salutation; LinkedIn does this automatically.

6. Click the Send button. LinkedIn sends your recommendation request to its target recipient. If you selected more than one person in step 2, each person receives an individual message.

See "Managing Recommendation Requests" to learn what happens when a connection receives your recommendation request.

Managing Recommendation Requests

After you send a recommendation request, the Received Recommendations tab indicates that you have a pending request. This text remains until your connection submits a recommendation for you.

To review your request, click the Manage link below the related position or school. The Manage Received Recommendations page opens, shown in Figure 10.3.

On this page, you can view a list of the recommendations you've requested and the date you requested them. If your request has been pending for more than a week, click the Resend link to send your request again with a message to the recipient. It's also a good idea to contact this person directly.

Received Recommendations	Sent Recommendations	Request Recommendations		

Recommendations for **Senior Account Executive at ABC Public Relations**

Pending recommendation requests

You've requested new or revised recommendations from these connections:

To	Message		Sent
Patrice-Anne Rutledge	Dear Patrice-Anne, I'm sending this to ask you...	[Resend]	May 28, 2009
Sara Wretstrom	Dear Sara, I'm following up on our phone...	[Resend]	September 6, 2010

FIGURE 10.3   Review your pending recommendation requests.

Responding to Recommendation Requests

LinkedIn sends a message to your Inbox when you receive recommendation requests. The default subject line for these messages is "Can You Endorse Me?" unless the person requesting the recommendation modifies this text.

To respond to a recommendation request, follow these steps:

1. On the global navigation bar, click the Inbox link. Refer to Lesson 6, "Communicating with Other LinkedIn Members," for more information about working with your Inbox.

2. Select the message that contains the recommendation request. Figure 10.4 illustrates a sample recommendation request.

3. Click the Write Recommendation button to write your recommendation. The Select Type page opens, shown in Figure 10.5.

> NOTE: **LinkedIn Handles Student Requests Differently**
> If this is for a student request, LinkedIn doesn't ask you to select a recommendation type and opens the Create Your Recommendation page directly.

4. If this recommendation is for a position, select from the following options: Colleague, Service Provider, or Business Partner. Refer to "Understanding LinkedIn Recommendations," earlier in this lesson, for more information about these recommendation types.

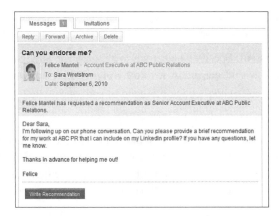

FIGURE 10.4   LinkedIn notifies you every time you receive a recommendation request.

FIGURE 10.5   Your options vary depending on the recommendation type you choose.

5. Click the Continue button to open the Create Your Recommendation page, shown in Figure 10.6.

6. Select a Basis of Recommendation from the drop-down list. Depending on the type of recommendation you're giving, these options could include

   ▶ **Colleague:** Specify whether you managed this person; reported to this person; were senior to this person, but didn't manage this person directly; held a lower position, but didn't report to this person; worked in the same group; or worked in different groups.

▶ **Business Partner:** Specify whether you worked together at different companies or whether the person was your client.

▶ **Student:** Specify whether you were a teacher, advisor, or fellow student.

7. Select your title at the time from the drop-down list, which includes the positions on your profile.

8. Enter your recommendation in the Written Recommendation box. LinkedIn offers sample text, but you need to replace this with your own recommendation. Write a concise, specific recommendation that relates to the position and the goals of the person you're recommending.

9. Click the View/Edit button to display the Personalize This Message text box, where you can personalize the message you send to the person requesting your recommendation. This text doesn't appear on the recommendation itself.

FIGURE 10.6 Create a recommendation that describes this person's accomplishments clearly and concisely.

10. Click the Send button to send the recommendation and accompanying message to the requestor.

TIP: **Consider Carefully Who You Recommend**

Consider carefully before recommending someone on LinkedIn. Remember that your reputation is based not only on who recommends you, but also on who you recommend. Is this someone you would recommend in the real world? If not, reply privately to the person explaining that you don't feel comfortable giving the recommendation. For example, you might not know the person well enough for a recommendation, or your experience working together might not have been a positive one.

Accepting Recommendations

When someone recommends you, LinkedIn sends you a notification message. If you indicate that you want to receive email notifications on the Account & Settings page, LinkedIn also notifies you by email.

Open the message to view the complete recommendation. Figure 10.7 illustrates a sample message.

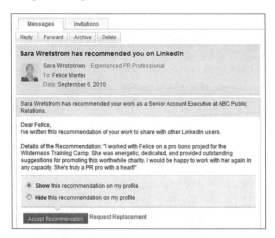

FIGURE 10.7   Review your recommendation for accuracy before accepting it.

On this page, you can

▶ Select Show This Recommendation on My Profile if you want to display the recommendation.

▶ Select Hide This Recommendation on My Profile if you want to hide the recommendation. In general, displaying your recommendations is a good promotional tool. You should hide unsolicited recommendations you don't want others to view.

▶ Click the Accept Recommendation button to accept the recommendation.

▶ Click the Request Replacement link to ask for a revised recommendation. This option is useful if the recommendation isn't accurate, contains misspellings, or doesn't focus on your current goals or accomplishments. To ensure you receive a more appropriate recommendation, be sure to specify *why* you need a replacement.

If you accept your recommendation and choose to show it on your profile, you can view it below its related position or school.

Making Recommendations

At times, you might want to recommend your connections even if they don't send you a recommendation request. To make a recommendation, follow these steps:

1. On the global navigation bar, select Recommendations from the Profile drop-down menu.

2. Scroll down the Received Recommendations page to the Make a Recommendation box, shown in Figure 10.8.

TIP: **Make Recommendations from a Connection's Profile Page**

Another way to initiate a recommendation is to visit a connection's profile page and click the Recommend link below the related position or school, which opens the Create Your Recommendation page.

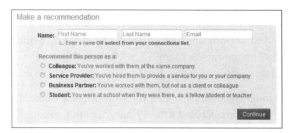

FIGURE 10.8   You can make several kinds of recommendations on
LinkedIn.

3. Click the Select from Your Connections List link to select your
target recipient. Alternatively, enter a person's name and email
address.

4. Select the type of recommendation you want to write. Options
include Colleague, Service Provider, Business Partner, and
Student. See Lesson 14, "Using LinkedIn Service Providers," for
more information about service provider recommendations.

5. Click the Continue button to open the Create Your
Recommendation page.

See "Responding to Recommendation Requests" earlier in this lesson for
more information on completing the Create Your Recommendation page.
The process is the same whether you respond to a recommendation request
or initiate it yourself.

Managing Recommendations

Several times a year, you should review your recommendations to verify
that they're still relevant to your current goals. You might want to hide a
recommendation that's no longer relevant or request updated recommendations from those who have recommended you in the past.

To manage your recommendations, select Recommendations from the
Profile drop-down menu on the global navigation bar.

Managing Received Recommendations

On the Received Recommendations page, click the Manage link below the recommendation you want to change. The Manage Received Recommendations page opens, shown in Figure 10.9.

To hide a recommendation from your profile, remove the check mark next to the Show check box. Click the Save Changes button to save this change.

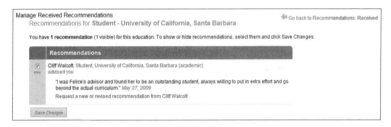

FIGURE 10.9   Review your recommendations regularly to verify that they still meet your needs.

To ask a connection for a revised recommendation, click the Request a New or Revised Recommendation From [Person's Name] link. LinkedIn sends a message to this connection asking for a revision. Be sure to communicate clearly what you're looking for in your revised recommendation. For example, you might want to revise a recommendation if your job duties for the same position have changed or you want to emphasize a different aspect of your job for future career growth.

TIP: **Request a New Recommendation If You Have a New Job Title**

If you receive a promotion or have a new job title, add a new position and request a recommendation for that job rather than revising an existing recommendation.

Managing Sent Recommendations

To manage the recommendations you give others, select Recommendations from the Profile drop-down menu on the global navigation bar. Click the Sent Recommendations link to open the Sent Recommendations page, shown in Figure 10.10.

FIGURE 10.10 Revise or withdraw a recommendation on the Sent Recommendations page.

On this page, you can

▶ **Change the display options for a recommendation:** By default, the recommendations you give your connections appear on your profile for all LinkedIn members to see. Click the Display on My Profile To drop-down list and choose either Connections Only or No One to change this.

▶ **Revise a recommendation:** Click the Edit link next to the recommendation you want to revise and make your changes on the Edit Your Recommendation page. Click the Send button to make your changes and notify your connection.

▶ **Withdraw a recommendation:** Click the Edit link next to the recommendation you want to withdraw. On the Edit Your Recommendation page, click the Withdraw This Recommendation link. A pop-up box asks you to confirm that you want to withdraw the recommendation.

Summary

In this lesson, you learned how to request, provide, and manage professional recommendations on LinkedIn.

LESSON 11
Participating in LinkedIn Groups

In this lesson, you learn how to participate on LinkedIn groups, manage your groups, and create your own group.

Understanding LinkedIn Groups

LinkedIn groups offer a way for like-minded individuals to share and discuss relevant topics related to the focus of the group. With LinkedIn groups, you can network and share ideas with industry peers, discover job leads and recruit quality talent, promote your career or business, and learn about a wide range of professional topics.

Remember, to maximize the publicity potential of LinkedIn groups, focus on visibility and sharing your expertise rather than overt sales or advertising.

LinkedIn groups take many forms. There are groups for alumni, associations, nonprofits, professional interests, corporations, general networking, conference attendees, and personal interests. Your group activity appears on the Group Updates section on your home page, providing additional visibility for your group actions and your groups.

LinkedIn imposes a limit of 50 group memberships per account holder. If you reach 50 groups and want to join another, you need to leave a group of which you're currently a member. Because of this limit, it's important to consider carefully which groups will provide you with the most value and help you meet your goals.

> NOTE: **LinkedIn Open Groups**
>
> In general, you must request to join a LinkedIn group to participate in it. However, LinkedIn is currently introducing open groups as another group option. The discussions on an open group are visible to all LinkedIn users and don't require you to join the group. Other benefits of open groups include search engine indexing and sharing on Facebook and Twitter. All existing groups will remain members-only unless the group owner chooses to change the group's status.

Joining a Group

One of the best ways to find a group to join is to search LinkedIn's Groups Directory. To search the directory for potential groups to join, follow these steps:

1. On the global navigation bar, select Groups Directory from the Groups drop-down menu. The Featured Groups page opens, shown in Figure 11.1.

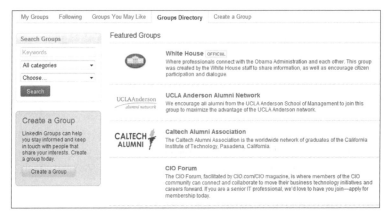

FIGURE 11.1   Join a featured group or search for one that meets your criteria.

TIP: **Let LinkedIn Suggest Groups for You**

Another way to find good groups is to let LinkedIn suggest groups for you. While viewing the Featured Groups page, click the Groups You May Like tab to view a list of groups LinkedIn suggests based on your profile content.

---

2. In the Search Groups box, enter keywords related to the group you want to find. For example, you could enter the name of a company, school, professional association, skill, or hobby.

3. If you want to narrow your search results by category, click All Categories and select a category from the drop-down list. Options include groups for professional association members, alumni, corporate employees, conference attendees, nonprofits, and general networking.

4. If you want to narrow your search by language, select a language from the Choose drop-down list.

5. Click the Search button to open the Search Results page, which displays a preview of each group that matches your search criteria. The preview boxes include a group description, the group owner's name, and the number of members. Click the group title to view more details, including a list of people in your network who already belong to this group.

NOTE: **Understanding Group Restrictions**

Although most groups are available to all LinkedIn members, be sure to clarify this in the group's description. Some groups, for example, require you to be an alumnus of a school or company, or to be a paid member of a professional association.

---

6. Click the Join Group button on the Search Results page to open the Join Group page, as shown in Figure 11.2.

FIGURE 11.2   Select your group contact preferences on the Join Group page.

7. If you want the group logo to appear in the Groups section on your profile, select the Group Logo check box. Placing this logo on your profile identifies you to fellow members.

8. Specify the Contact Email for sending group announcements and updates.

9. If you want to receive an email for each new discussion, select the Posts check box. Be aware that this could result in a lot of email if your group is an active one.

10. If you want to receive summary email updates of group activity, select the Digest Email check box. You can choose to have updates delivered on a daily basis or a weekly basis.

NOTE: **View Group Updates Online**

Even if you don't want to receive email notifications, you can keep up with your groups on LinkedIn. Your home page displays group updates, and the Updates tab on each group's page summarizes the latest activity as well.

---

11. To receive group announcements no more than once per week, select the Announcements check box.

12. To allow other members of your group to send you messages on LinkedIn, select the Messages check box. (They won't see your personal email address.)

13. Click the Join Group button to join the group.

The My Groups page opens, which lists your current and pending groups. Group managers approve join requests manually unless the group was set up for automatic approval. Your status for a new group on the My Groups page is listed as *pending approval*. This status remains until the group manager approves you. If you want to follow up with the group owner about a join request, click the Send Message to the Group Manager link. If want to cancel your request to join the group, click the Withdraw Request link.

Participating in Group Discussions

Participating in discussions is one of the greatest values of joining a group. With LinkedIn group discussions, you can view discussion threads for relevant professional information, add a comment to a current discussion, start your own discussion, or share news and links with group members.

CAUTION: **Focus on Quality, Professional Discussions**

As with everything else on LinkedIn, focus on intelligent, meaningful comments that add value to a discussion. Don't post a sales pitch or irrelevant comment just to lead people to your profile.

To view discussions for a group you belong to, click the Groups link on the global navigation menu to open the My Groups page. From there, click the title of the group you want to view. Near the top of the Discussion tab, the discussions carousel (see Figure 11.3) rotates new discussion content every few seconds. This is a great way to preview what's new with your group.

FIGURE 11.3   Preview a rotating carousel of new discussion content.

Below each carousel item, you'll find buttons that enable you to like the discussion (similar to Facebook's Like feature), add a comment, or flag the post as promotional, job-related, or inappropriate. To view a discussion item in more detail, click its headline.

The most popular discussions display below the carousel. Again, click a discussion item's headline to view the entire discussion, like it, add comments, follow it, flag it, or reply privately to the author.

Liking a Discussion

If you find a discussion item particularly useful and interesting, you can show your support by clicking the Like button below it in the discussion carousel or on its detail page (see Figure 11.4). Liking a discussion alerts other group members as well as your followers that you found the discussion worthwhile. If you change your mind or click this button by mistake, you can unlike the discussion.

FIGURE 11.4   Click the Like button to point out quality discussions to your fellow group members.

Adding Comments to a Discussion

To add a comment to a discussion, follow these steps:

1. Click the Comment button below any discussion item in the carousel. Alternatively, click the discussion headline to open it fully and comment on that page.

2. Enter your own comment in the Add a Comment text box, shown in Figure 11.5.

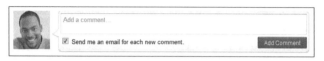

FIGURE 11.5   Contributing your own thoughts to a discussion.

3. If you want to receive email notification of any new comments in this discussion, select the Send Me an Email for Each New Comment check box.

4. Click the Add Comment button to post your comment.

> TIP: **Reply Privately If You Don't Want to Post a Comment**
>
> To reply privately to the original poster or anyone who posted a comment, select Reply Privately from the More drop-down menu.

After you post a comment, LinkedIn gives you 15 minutes to revise it. Click the Edit Comment link below your comment to make any changes. Click the Delete link to remove your comment from the discussion at any time.

Following Group Discussions and Members

If you want to know when someone adds a new comment to a discussion item you find particularly relevant, you can follow the discussion. To do so, click the discussion item's headline and click the Follow link below the discussion text on the detail page. LinkedIn sends you an email anytime someone adds a comment. By default, you follow any discussion that you start or comment on unless you specify that you don't want to receive email notification.

If you decide you no longer want to follow a discussion, click the Unfollow link below it. You can also manage your group-following activity by clicking a group's Following tab to open the My Followed Discussions page.

To follow a group member, click the Follow link below that person's photo. You can unfollow people by clicking the Stop Following link below their name or by going to the My Followed Discussions page.

Starting a Discussion

On the Discussions tab, you can start your own discussion or share relevant news and links with other group members.

To start your own discussion, follow these steps:

1. Enter up to 200 characters in the text box at the top of the Discussions tab (to the right of your photo), shown in Figure 11.6. This text serves as your discussion headline, so consider carefully what you want to enter.

FIGURE 11.6   Start a discussion or share some news.

2. The section expands to include a second text box where you can add more details (up to 4,000 characters).

3. If you want to refer to an external URL, click the Attach a Link link. If not, skip to step 9.

TIP: **You Can Attach a Link Without Entering Additional Text**

You can attach a link without posting anything in the discussion text boxes. When someone clicks your discussion headline, the LinkedIn action bar displays at the top of the screen and the page you linked to opens immediately.

---

4. Enter the URL you want to include in the Add News box, such as http://www.quepublishing.com. For example, you could attach a link to an article you just read in a major newspaper, or you could submit a great post from your favorite blog.

CAUTION: **Don't Overdo Self-Promotion**

Submitting your own articles, blog posts, or media coverage is acceptable, but don't overdo this feature as a promotional tool. Submit only the most informative, meaningful content that offers value to the members of your group. If your post is promotional, click the Promotions tab to post a promotion to your group.

---

5. Click the Attach button. LinkedIn searches for this URL and displays a title, description, and photo from this content it finds on this page (see Figure 11.7).

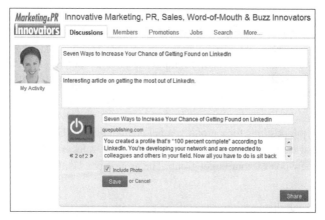

FIGURE 11.7 Attach links to relevant external sites, such as a website, blog, or news site.

6. Optionally, click the Edit link to make changes to this default content.

7. Enter any changes to the title or description in the text boxes.

8. The Include Photo check box is selected by default, but you can remove this check mark if you don't want to include a photo. To change from the default photo, click the arrows below the photo to view alternative selections. LinkedIn searches for any photos on the page you're sharing and offers them as options.

9. Click the Share button to post your discussion item for your fellow group members to see.

Using a Group's Jobs Discussion Board

If you're recruiting for a position that would interest the members of a specific LinkedIn group, you can post your job on the group's Jobs Discussion Board, located on the Jobs tab. This is also a great place for job seekers to find targeted jobs.

> TIP: **Consider LinkedIn's Other Job Search and Recruiting Tools**
>
> For more ways to search for and post jobs on LinkedIn, click the Jobs link on the top navigation menu. Refer to Lesson 9, "Finding a Job," and Web Lesson 1, "Recruiting Job Candidates," for more information.

To view job postings for a group you belong to, click the Groups link on the global navigation bar. On the My Groups page, select Go To, Jobs in the preview box of your target group. The group opens with the Jobs tab selected.

The Jobs tab displays a preview of the jobs with the most recent activity. Each preview box includes the name and photo of the person who posted the job, when it was posted, and links to follow the discussion or add comments.

Although Recent Activity is the default view, you can also click any of the links on the left side of the page for additional views.

To view the actual job posting, click the job headline. The links below the job description text enable you to like the job posting, comment on it, follow it, flag it, or reply privately to the poster. These functions are very similar to responding to a discussion item, covered in the "Participating in Group Discussions" section earlier in this lesson.

To post a job, follow these steps:

1. Select the Jobs tab and click the Post a Job link. The Post a Job page opens, shown in Figure 11.8.

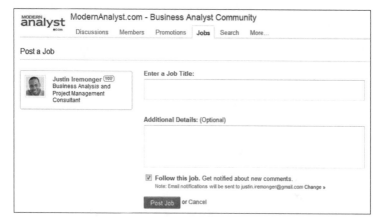

FIGURE 11.8   Post a job targeted to members of a specific LinkedIn group.

2. Enter a job title that clearly defines the nature of the job.

3. Enter additional details about your job. If you don't want potential candidates to contact you through LinkedIn, be sure to provide alternative contact information.

4. If you want to receive email notification of any new comments related to the job you post, select the Follow This Job check box.

5. Click the Post Job button to post your job to the Jobs tab.

Managing Your Groups

LinkedIn offers you lots of flexibility in how you participate in, manage, and view the groups you join. You can also search for and share specific group information, and leave a group any time you want.

Viewing Your Groups

You can view a list of the groups you belong to by clicking the Groups link on the global navigation bar. The My Groups page opens, shown in Figure 11.9.

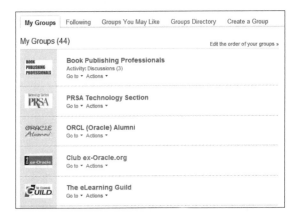

FIGURE 11.9 View information about all your groups in one place.

This page lists all your groups with the following links appearing below each group's name:

▶ **Go To:** Click the Go To link and select one of the following options from the drop-down list: Discussions, Subgroups, Jobs, Updates, Members, or Settings.

▶ **Actions:** Click the Actions link and select one of the following actions: Forward, Start a Discussion, or Leave Group.

If your request to join a group is still pending, you'll see a notification in that group's preview box. The links to specific tasks aren't available until you're approved for a group. If you are not yet approved, your options include emailing the group manager or withdrawing your request.

If you're the group manager, a Manage link is also available.

TIP: **View Your Group Information on Your Profile**
You can also view a list of the groups you belong to on your profile.

Changing the Display Order of Your Groups

For easy access to your groups, LinkedIn displays the first three groups in your My Groups list on the Groups menu you access from the global navigation bar (see Figure 11.10).

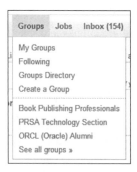

| Groups | Jobs | Inbox (154) |

My Groups
Following
Groups Directory
Create a Group

Book Publishing Professionals
PRSA Technology Section
ORCL (Oracle) Alumni
See all groups »

FIGURE 11.10   Access your favorite groups directly from your home page.

If you're a frequent participant in group activity, it's a good idea to display your favorite groups on this navigation menu. You can also increase the number of displayed groups from 3 to as many as 10.

To change the display order of your groups, follow these steps:

1. On the global navigation bar, click the Groups link.

2. On the My Groups page, click the Edit the Order of Your Groups link. The Groups Order and Display page opens, shown in Figure 11.11.

My Groups	Following	Groups You May Like	Groups Directory	Create a Group

Groups Order and Display

Choose which groups display in what order in the main navigation.

Groups (44)

Display the first `3 ▾` groups in the navigation. (Pending groups will not show up)

Order		Group Name
1		Book Publishing Professionals
2	⌕	PRSA Technology Section
3	⌕	ORCL (Oracle) Alumni
4	⌕	Club ex-Oracle.org
5	⌕	The eLearning Guild
6	⌕	Global eLearning Community
7	⌕	Consultants Network
8	⌕	UCI Alumni
9	⌕	Web 2.0

FIGURE 11.11   Choosing the order in which your groups appear.

3. Select the number of group links to display on the Groups drop-down menu on the global navigation bar. Options range from 1 to 10.

4. Use the Order field to move each of your groups up or down until you reach your desired display order.

NOTE: **Change Your Settings for Each of Your Groups**

You can specify different settings for each of your groups. Click the Member Settings link to make changes to a particular group. See "Managing Group Settings" later in this lesson for more information.

---

5. Click the Save Changes button to save your changes, which appear on the navigation menu.

Viewing Group Updates

To view the latest group updates, pause your mouse over the More tab on any group page and then select Updates from the drop-down list. The Updates page lists activity for the current and previous day, such as who joined the group, who started a discussion, who posted comments, and so forth. The default view is All Updates. Click the People I'm Following tab to display updates only from those group members you follow.

Viewing Group Members

To view a list of group members, click the Members tab on any group page. This page tells you how many members a group has and displays previews of each group member, starting with you. From there, LinkedIn lists your 1st degree connections, your 2nd degree connections, and, finally, all other members.

Depending on members' settings and connection to you, their preview could include a photo, a profile link, a professional headline, their number of connections, and links to connect and send a message.

To search a group's member list for members matching specific criteria, enter keywords in the Search Members box and click the Search button. You can also search groups from the quick search box on the top navigation menu. Refer to Lesson 7, "Searching on LinkedIn," for more information on searching for people.

Managing Group Settings

To revise your settings for a group, pause your mouse over the More tab on any group page and then select My Settings from the drop-down list. The Settings page opens, which gives you the option to modify the visibility and contact options for a specific group.

The Settings page is identical to the Join a Group page. Refer to "Joining a Group," earlier in this lesson, for more information on the settings you can modify on this page.

Forwarding Information About Groups

If you're a member of a particular group that you think your connections would also enjoy, let them know about it by clicking the Forward This Group link on the Discussions tab of any group.

LinkedIn takes you to your Inbox where you can send a group link to as many as 50 of your connections. For best results, let your connections know why you recommend this group or why it's appropriate for them.

See Lesson 6, "Communicating with Other LinkedIn Members," for more information about the Inbox and sending messages.

Leaving a Group

If you decide that a group no longer meets your needs or you have to pare down your current group membership to make room for new groups, you can easily leave a group.

To do so, select Action, Leave Group on the My Groups page. LinkedIn displays a pop-up box asking you to confirm that you want to leave the group. Click the Yes, Leave Group button to remove the group from your My Groups page.

Creating and Managing Your Own Group

Creating your own group is a good way to develop a community for a topic, profession, or interest. Before you create a group, consider the following:

- ▶ Is there already a similar group on LinkedIn Groups? If so, how will your group differ? What value will you add?

- ▶ Is your proposed group an advertisement in disguise? Although many LinkedIn members do benefit from their participation with LinkedIn groups, you need to create a group whose focus is providing value and community to its members. If you don't, your group most likely won't succeed.

- ▶ Do you have the time to maintain and support your group? If you don't respond quickly to join requests and keep the activity going with your group, it won't flourish.

Creating Your Own Group

To create a new LinkedIn group, follow these steps:

   1. On the global navigation bar, click the Groups link.

2. On the My Groups page, click the Create a Group link. The Create a Group page opens, shown in Figure 11.12.

FIGURE 11.12   Creating your own group.

3. Click the Browse button in the Logo section to select and upload a logo for your group. Supported formats include PNG, JPEG, and GIF files no larger than 100KB.

4. Enter a group name. If your group also exists outside of LinkedIn, you can increase visibility by including the actual group name rather than just an acronym. For example, enter International Association of Business Communicators (IABC) instead of only IABC.

5. Select a group type. Options include alumni, corporate, conference, networking, nonprofit, professional, or other groups. The Other group type is most appropriate for special interest or hobby groups that don't fit into any other category.

6. Enter a summary of your group. In this text box, indicate your group's focus, goals, and any membership benefits your group might provide for LinkedIn members. This summary appears in the Groups Directory.

7. In the Description text box, enter more details to display on your group pages.

8. If your group has an external website, enter the URL in the Website field.

9. Enter the Group Owner Email. LinkedIn sends all messages about your group to this email address.

10. If you want to approve group membership requests, select the Request to Join option button. This option is selected by default. LinkedIn sends a message whenever someone requests to join your group, and you must approve the request manually. This requires extra effort on your part, but it ensures that only qualified people join your group. If your group members work for the same organization, you can pre-approve members with a specific email domain by entering it in the text box below.

11. If you want LinkedIn to approve new group members automatically, without your approval, select the Open Access option button.

12. Select the Display This Group in the Groups Directory check box or the Allow Group Members to Display the Logo on Their Profiles check box if you want to enable these options. These are great promotional tools for your group. Unless you have a specific need for privacy, it's a good idea to make your group visible.

13. Select a language for your group. English is the default language for groups, but LinkedIn offers numerous language choices.

14. If your group is for members who are located in a specific geographic location, select the Location check box. The Country and Postal Code fields appear so that you can specify the exact location of your group.

15. If you agree to the Terms of Service, select the Agreement check box. The Terms of Service cover your rights to provide LinkedIn with the email addresses of group members and LinkedIn's rights to use the logo you upload.

16. Click the Create Group button to create your group.

LinkedIn reviews your request to create a new group and approves the group if it meets LinkedIn's guidelines.

Managing Your Own Group

After LinkedIn approves your group, you can start inviting and accepting members.

As a reminder, click the Groups link on the global navigation bar to open the My Groups page where you can access all your LinkedIn groups. To manage your group, select the Manage tab on your group's page.

On the Manage tab, you can

- ► Approve or reject requests to join your group.

- ► Send invitations to LinkedIn members asking them to join your group.

- ► Upload a pre-approved list of email addresses for your group in the CSV format. This option is useful if your group also exists outside of LinkedIn, and you know the members you want to pre-approve.

> TIP: **Create Your CSV File in Microsoft Excel**
>
> Enter your list of pre-approved members in an Excel file with columns for first name, last name, and email. Save your spreadsheet as a CSV file. CSV stands for *comma separated values*, a common text file format.

Summary

In this lesson, you learned how to join and participate in LinkedIn groups, create your own groups, and manage your own groups.

LESSON 12

Using LinkedIn Answers

In this lesson, you learn how to ask and answer questions that give you valuable feedback from the LinkedIn community and develop your reputation as an expert in your field.

Understanding LinkedIn Answers

LinkedIn Answers is an interactive feature that enables you to ask questions, receive input from a worldwide network of peers and experts, share your own expertise, and develop your platform as an expert.

CAUTION: **LinkedIn Answers Is for Professional Discussion, Not Promotion**

Understand that LinkedIn Answers is for genuine information sharing among professional peers. It's not the place for sales pitches (overt or disguised), open requests for help in getting a job, and so forth. That said, asking intelligent, relevant questions and providing useful answers with real value can help develop your expert image on LinkedIn.

To view questions and answers, select Answers from the More drop-down menu on the global navigation bar. The Answers page opens, shown in Figure 12.1.

On the Answers Home tab, you can view the following:

> ► A box with shortcuts for asking and answering questions. LinkedIn recommends up to five categories based on previous questions you've answered. If you haven't answered questions, this section displays the Answer Now button.

▶ A list of recent questions from your network.

▶ The week's top experts, based on the number of questions they've answered and the number of times their answers have been selected as best answers.

▶ The My Q&A box listing your open questions, if any.

▶ A complete list of LinkedIn Answers categories.

▶ Links to questions in French, Spanish, German, Italian, and Portuguese, as well as English.

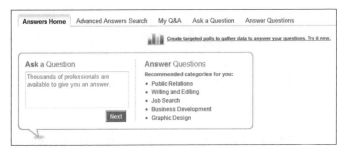

FIGURE 12.1   Participate in the LinkedIn community by asking and answering questions.

You can ask and answer questions that relate to professional topics in more than 20 categories, including Management, Marketing and Sales, Professional Development, Finance and Accounting, Technology, and more.

Your activity on LinkedIn Answers also appears in the Q & A box on your profile, shown in Figure 12.2.

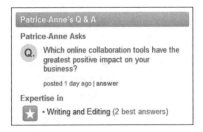

FIGURE 12.2   Your profile promotes your activity on LinkedIn Answers.

This box lists your questions, answers, and expertise. If you've received any best-answer votes, a green square with a white star appears in this box. To remove the Q & A box from your profile, click the Change This Setting link. For example, if you answer questions that don't relate to your professional experience, you might not want to display these on your profile.

Asking a Question

LinkedIn members with at least five connections can ask as many as 10 questions a month on LinkedIn Answers. LinkedIn imposes a limit to avoid the problem of "question spam" and to encourage members to ask questions of value to the LinkedIn community.

To ask a question:

1. Select Answers from the More drop-down menu on the global navigation bar.

2. Click the Ask a Question tab to open the Ask a Question page, shown in Figure 12.3.

FIGURE 12.3   Ask a question to tap into the insight of LinkedIn's millions of members.

> TIP: **Take a Shortcut in Asking a Question**
> You can also ask your question in the Ask a Question box on the LinkedIn Answers Home tab. When you click Next, LinkedIn takes you to the Ask a Question tab where you can complete your question.

3. In the first text box, enter a one-line question. Make sure your question is clear and concise. Vague, open-ended questions rarely receive good feedback. For example, asking LinkedIn members for suggestions on online invoicing applications suited to a small business is a good, focused question. Asking members how to make lots of money with your new website, which you promote in the details section, is not the way to use LinkedIn Answers.

4. If you want to send your question only to specific people (up to 200 of your connections), select the Only Share This Question with Connections I Select check box. For maximum response and visibility, it's best to post your question to the public LinkedIn Answers section.

5. In the Add Details box, provide pertinent background information to clarify your question further. Be careful, however, of adding too much detail. Although you can add content up to 2,000 characters, many people skip over lengthy questions.

6. Categorize your question based on the available categories and subcategories. You can add a second category if desired.

7. If your question is location-specific, select the My Question Is Focused Around a Specific Geographic Location check box. LinkedIn asks you to select a country and postal code, if applicable.

8. Specify whether your question relates to one of the following: recruiting, promoting your services, or job seeking.

> NOTE: **Alternatives to LinkedIn Answers**
> If your question relates to recruiting, promotion, or a job search, LinkedIn offers links to other features that might be more appropri-

ate than LinkedIn Answers. For example, consider posting a job using LinkedIn Jobs or promoting your services in LinkedIn Service Providers directory instead.

9. Click the Ask Question button to post your question.

LinkedIn's millions of members now have the opportunity to view and answer your question, providing valuable feedback and information.

LinkedIn automatically closes your question in seven days, but offers you the choice to extend the question another week or close it manually before seven days. See the section "Viewing and Modifying Your Questions and Answers" later in this lesson for more information.

One final step is to select a best answer to the question you posted, if you feel one response provided the most value. LinkedIn members who receive the best answer designations are recognized in the LinkedIn Answers list of experts and on their profiles.

Browsing Open Questions to Answer

In addition to viewing questions to answer on the Answers Home tab, you can find more questions on the Answer Questions tab. When you select this tab, the Browse Open Questions page opens. Question summaries appear in the order of their author's connection to you. For example, questions from your 1st degree connections appear first, and so forth. Click the Date link to sort questions by date instead.

TIP: **Answer Questions in LinkedIn's Recommended Categories**

On the Answers Home tab, LinkedIn recommends question categories for you based on your profile and any questions you've previously answered.

Figure 12.4 shows a sample question summary.

FIGURE 12.4   To elicit the best responses, ask clear, concise questions.

In addition to the question title, LinkedIn displays the number of answers the question has received, its author, the date it was posted, and its categories.

To browse questions relating to a specific category, click one of the links in the Browse box on the right side of your screen. Most categories have subcategories you can use to narrow the subject matter of posted questions.

TIP: **Subscribe to an RSS Feed to Stay Informed**

If you're interested in questions related to a specific category, you can subscribe to the RSS feed for that category by clicking the link next to the orange and white feed icon at the bottom of the Browse box. LinkedIn opens the Subscribe Now pop-up box, which enables you to subscribe using your favorite feed reader (such as My Yahoo! or Google Reader). Refer to Lesson 4, "Customizing Your LinkedIn Settings," for more information about subscribing to RSS feeds.

You can also browse questions in a specific language. LinkedIn enables members to post questions in English, French, Spanish, German, Italian, and Portuguese.

Finally, the Browse Open Questions page also offers links for viewing closed questions and popular experts.

NOTE: **Reporting Problem Questions**

If you view a question that you feel is inappropriate, click the Report Question As link below it to alert LinkedIn staff. Potential reasons for reporting a question include duplicate questions, open

advertising, recruitment messages, inappropriate content, connec-
tion-building spam, or misrepresentation.

Answering Questions

To post a public reply to a question, follow these steps:

1. Click the question title link to view the question's details. Figure
   12.5 illustrates a sample question.

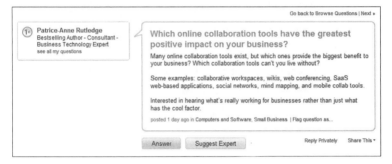

FIGURE 12.5 You can answer questions publicly or privately.

2. Click the Answer button to expand the Your Answer box, shown
   in Figure 12.6.

Your Answer
Your answer will be visible to all LinkedIn users.

Web Resources (optional)

List websites that support your answer (ex: http://www.site.com)

List websites that support your answer (ex: http://www.site.com)

List websites that support your answer (ex: http://www.site.com)

Suggest an Expert (optional)

Select Experts from your network

FIGURE 12.6 You can include up to three web links with your answer.

3. Enter your answer in the text box. Remember to provide value and true information. Don't sell your own expertise and services. Let your LinkedIn profile do that for you.

4. Optionally, list up to three web resources. Include the complete URL, such as http://www.patricerutledge.com.

5. Optionally, click the Suggest Expert button to open your connection list. You can choose up to three experts from your network to recommend for this question. The experts you suggest appear in your answer with links to their profiles.

6. Enter an optional, private note to the person who posted the question. No other LinkedIn members will see this content.

7. Enter the characters that display in the text box to verify that you're a real person answering a question.

8. Click Submit to post your answer.

If you don't want to answer a question directly, you can

▶ Click the Suggest Expert button to choose expert referrals from your list of connections.

▶ Click the Reply Privately link to send a private message to the person who posted the question.

▶ Click the Share This link to email this question to others or post to the social bookmarking site Delicious. This is a good way to expand the visibility of LinkedIn questions.

When you answer a question, it's important to provide an intelligent, helpful response. Responding to numerous questions with vague answers in an effort to increase your visibility won't pay off in the long run. Focus on quality rather than quantity and answer only when you have something meaningful to contribute.

LinkedIn members who post questions can award a best-answer designation to the person who provides the most helpful answer. When you receive Best Answer votes, you increase your ranking on the list of experts.

Searching LinkedIn Answers by Keyword

LinkedIn's advanced search functionality lets you search its vast collection of questions and answers for specific information.

Searching by keyword enables you to

▶ Find specific questions to answer

▶ Discover solutions to your own professional questions from LinkedIn's large collection of information

▶ Determine what people are asking and saying about you, your company, or your products

▶ Collect competitive intelligence

To search by keyword:

1. Click the Advanced Answers Search tab on the Answers page. Figure 12.7 shows your search possibilities.

FIGURE 12.7   Search LinkedIn Answers for specific keywords.

2. In the Keywords field, enter your search terms. The more specific your keywords, the more targeted your results will be.

TIP: **Take Advantage of Advanced Search Techniques**

To search on a specific phrase, use quotation marks (such as "social media" to search specifically for social media). Refer to Lesson 7, "Searching on LinkedIn," for more information about advanced searching techniques.

3. Specify whether you want to search in questions and answers or questions only.

4. Select a category and related subcategory in the Category field.

5. If you want to view only questions that haven't been answered, select the Show Only Unanswered Questions check box.

6. Click the Search button to display search results.

To view only open questions, click the Open Questions tab. From this page, you can also further refine your search criteria if necessary.

TIP: **Search LinkedIn Answers from the Quick Search Box**

You can also search LinkedIn Answers from the quick search box on the global navigation bar. Select Answers from the drop-down list, enter your keywords, and click the Search button. Or click the Advanced Link to open the Advanced Answers Search tab.

Viewing and Modifying Your Questions and Answers

To view and modify your own activity on LinkedIn Answers, click the My Q&A tab on the Answers page.

On the first tab, My Questions, LinkedIn displays a summary of the questions you've asked. Click the link of any question to view it; if the question is still open, you can revise it. Figure 12.8 shows a sample open question.

If the question is still open, you can

▶ Click the Forward This Question link to send the question to up to 200 of your connections.

Go back to My Questions

Your question closes in **7 days**:
* Forward this question

Close Question Now

Which ereader will hold the largest market share five years from now?

Looking for insight, predictions, and commentary.

posted 37 seconds ago in Wireless | Clarify my question

Share This ▾

FIGURE 12.8   You can modify a question that's still open.

▶ Click the Close Question Now button to close the question before it closes automatically in seven days. You can also hide your closed question from public view. For maximum visibility, it's best to keep your question open and allow it to remain on LinkedIn Answers. If you make a mistake or no longer want to display your question, however, you can close and hide it.

▶ Click the Clarify My Question link, below the question itself, to open the Clarify Your Question page and add related details. LinkedIn doesn't allow you to edit the question you posted.

▶ Click the Share This link to share your question by email or on the social bookmarking site Delicious.

On the second tab, My Answers, LinkedIn displays summaries of all the questions you've answered. The right side of this page lists the categories in which you've demonstrated expertise (based on receiving "best answer" ratings), your answer ratings for closed questions, and statistics about your activity on LinkedIn Answers.

You can modify or delete your answers to open questions only. Click the Clarify My Answer link to add clarification to your existing answer. Click the Delete My Answer link to delete your answer.

Summary

In this lesson, you learned how to maximize the potential of LinkedIn Answers for finding professional solutions, demonstrating your expertise, and interacting with a worldwide audience of millions.

LESSON 13

Using LinkedIn Applications

In this lesson, you learn how to enhance your LinkedIn experience with LinkedIn applications, including how to add, manage, and remove these applications.

Understanding LinkedIn Applications

LinkedIn Applications are optional extensions to LinkedIn that enhance the content and effectiveness of your profile, foster collaboration with your network, and integrate your LinkedIn data with other sites to provide further research and competitive intelligence opportunities.

The following LinkedIn applications are currently available, with more in development:

- ▶ Blog Link by SixApart
- ▶ Box.net Files by Box.net
- ▶ Company Buzz by LinkedIn
- ▶ Events by LinkedIn
- ▶ FT Press Delivers by FT Press
- ▶ Google Presentation by Google
- ▶ Huddle Workspaces by Huddle.net
- ▶ Lawyer Ratings by LexisNexis Martindale-Hubbell

- ► Legal Updates by JD Supra

- ► My Travel by TripIt

- ► Polls by LinkedIn

- ► Portfolio Display by Behance

- ► Projects and Teamspaces by Manymoon

- ► Reading List by Amazon

- ► Real Estate Pro by Rofo

- ► SAP Community Bio by LinkedIn

- ► SlideShare Presentations by SlideShare

- ► Tweets by LinkedIn

- ► WordPress by WordPress

All LinkedIn applications are free, but some require you to have an account with an application that might charge fees based on your usage. For example, Box.net Files and Huddle Workspaces offer both free and fee-based plans.

Choosing the Right Applications

LinkedIn applications offer many options for sharing and collaborating. At times, the number of choices is overwhelming. Although some applications, such as My Travel and Company Buzz, are unique in terms of the features they provide, other applications overlap in their functionality. For example, both Blog Link and WordPress enable you to share blog posts on your profile. You can share presentations using Google Presentation, SlideShare Presentations, and even Box.net Files.

Here are some tips for making the most of LinkedIn applications:

- ► Analyze how each application fits into your strategic plan and helps you meet your goals. Just because something sounds interesting doesn't make it worthwhile to add.

▶ If more than one application performs the same function, com-
pare their features before you pick one to use. Fortunately,
LinkedIn applications are easy to add and remove.

▶ Focus on quality rather than quantity when choosing the documents and presentations you would like to share. A resume, portfolio, or presentation that highlights your business can enhance
the effectiveness and reach of your LinkedIn profile, but don't add
so many documents that the important ones are lost in the mix.

▶ Consider your personal privacy with all the documents and data
you share online. For example, adding your resume to your profile can aid in your job search, but you might not want to include
your home address or phone number.

▶ Determine whether you have the legal right to post presentations
or other documents you created for an employer.

Adding Applications

To add an application to your profile or home page, follow these steps:

1. On the global navigation bar, select Get More Applications from
the More drop-down list. Alternatively, click the Add an
Application link on the bottom of the Edit Profile page. The
Applications page opens (see Figure 13.1).

2. Select the application you want to add. The page for that application opens. Figure 13.2 illustrates the Google Presentation page,
as an example.

3. The Application Info box appears on the right side of every
application page. In this box, choose whether you want to display
the application on your profile, on your LinkedIn home page, or
on both.

4. Click the Add Application button to add the application and enter
details specific to that application.

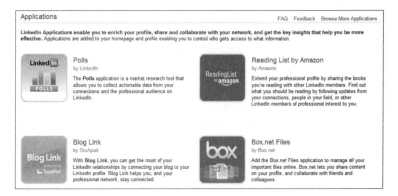

FIGURE 13.1   Enhance your LinkedIn experience with one of the many available applications.

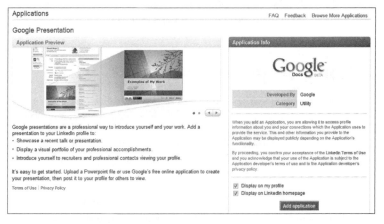

FIGURE 13.2   Google Presentation is one of many LinkedIn applications.

The rest of this section explains how to set up individual applications. This lesson provides detailed instructions for only the most popular applications, not every available application.

When you add an application, a link to it appears on the More drop-down menu on the global navigation bar. If you haven't added any applications, only the Reading List by Amazon and Events links appear by default.

Adding the Blog Link Application

The Blog Link application enables you to post summaries of your blog posts to your LinkedIn profile. You can also follow the blog posts of LinkedIn members in your network. Blog Link supports blogs on multiple platforms including TypePad, Movable Type, Vox, Wordpress.com, Wordpress.org, Blogger, LiveJournal, and more.

> NOTE: **If You Use WordPress, Consider the WordPress Application**
>
> WordPress users have two choices for displaying their blog posts on their profiles: the Blog Link application and the WordPress application. Both applications serve the same function, but they display your blog posts in a different format. If you use WordPress, try both applications to see which one you prefer. See "Adding the WordPress Application" later in this lesson for more information.

Before adding the Blog Link application, verify that the URL to your blog appears in the Websites section on your profile. Refer to Lesson 2, "Creating Your Profile," for more information on listing your blog in this section. The application pulls your blog data from your profile and doesn't work properly if you don't have a listed blog.

To add the Blog Link application, follow the steps listed in "Adding Applications" earlier in this lesson, selecting the Blog Link application on the Applications page. The Blog Link application opens.

The Blog Link application searches for your blog posts and includes summaries on your LinkedIn profile (see Figure 13.3). They also appear on the By Me tab in the Blog Link application.

> CAUTION: **What to Do If Your Blog Posts Don't Appear on Your Profile**
>
> If your blog posts don't appear on your profile, verify that you selected the Display on My Profile check box on the initial application page. Also, verify that your blog is listed on the Websites section of your profile. The Blog Link application pulls its content from the blog listed in this section.

FIGURE 13.3   Automatically post your blog updates to your LinkedIn profile.

Blog Link also searches for blog posts from your connections and includes these on the From My Contacts tab. If you don't want to view a particular blog, click the Hide This Feed link below its title. Blog posts from other LinkedIn members don't appear on your profile.

CAUTION: **Only Add Blogs That Relate to Your Professional Activities**

Remember that your LinkedIn profile is part of your professional presence online. Include only blog content that supports your professional image. Personal blogs or blogs covering controversial topics might not be suitable to share with your LinkedIn connections.

Adding the Box.net Files Application

The Box.net Files application enables you to share content from Box.net (www.box.net), a leading online collaboration and file-sharing website. With this application, you can post files such as resumes, portfolios, and presentations to your profile, collaborate privately with your LinkedIn connections, and view and edit your files online.

To add the Box.net Files application, follow the steps listed in the "Adding Applications" section earlier in this lesson, selecting the Box.net Files application on the Applications page.

The Box.net Files application opens, requesting that you log in to your Box.net Files account or sign up for a free account.

After you log in, you can upload files, view your connections' public files, and collaborate privately with your connections.

The files you selected to display publicly on your profile appear in the Applications section, shown in Figure 13.4.

FIGURE 13.4   Posting your resume can help you stand out from the crowd of other job seekers.

Adding a Poll

The Polls application enables you to poll LinkedIn users about relevant professional topics and participate in polls other LinkedIn members create. A LinkedIn poll is a short question with the option of providing as many as five answers. Members select their preferred answer and the Polls application tallies the results. Polls are different from other applications in that they don't integrate with external data and they offer both free and fee-based options.

You can invite your 1ˢᵗ degree connections on LinkedIn to participate in your poll at no charge or purchase a paid poll that surveys a wider audience on LinkedIn. If you choose to purchase a paid poll, you can specify a target audience based on job function, seniority, gender, age, or geography. You pay a set fee of $1 per response with a minimum purchase of 50 responses. If you're a LinkedIn premium member, you might be eligible for discounts or special offers.

To create a poll, follow these steps:

1. Follow the steps listed in the "Adding Applications" section earlier in this lesson, selecting the Polls application on the Applications page. The Create a Poll page opens, shown in Figure 13.5. If you already installed the Polls application, you can select it from the More drop-down menu on the global navigation bar.

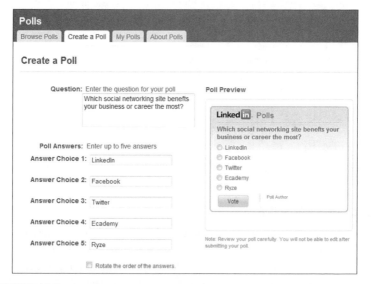

FIGURE 13.5   Use a LinkedIn poll to gain valuable insight and perform market research.

2. Enter a question of no more than 75 characters.

3. Enter up to five possible answers (using no more than 40 characters per answer) to your question.

TIP: **Review the Poll Preview Box for Accuracy**

Review the Poll Preview box to ensure that your poll is accurate. You can't edit it after submitting, so be careful to avoid spelling, grammar, or content errors.

---

4. Click the Rotate the Order of the Answers check box if you want to vary the position of your answers in your poll.

5. Select the audience for your poll's distribution. Options include

▶ **Target Audience of Professionals in the U.S:** With this option, you can select a target audience and receive a guaranteed response for a fee.

▶ **Your 1ˢᵗ Degree Connections:** LinkedIn sends a network update informing your connections about your poll. The number of responses you receive will vary based on your number of connections and their interest in participating in your poll. LinkedIn will also provide you with a URL you can use to share your poll with others.

TIP: **Gain Added Visibility in the LinkedIn Polls Directory**

Optionally, you can select the Visibility check box to include your free poll in the LinkedIn Polls directory where anyone on LinkedIn can view it and respond.

---

6. Click the Post Poll button to post your poll to the Network Activity section on your connections' home page. If you selected the fee-based poll option, LinkedIn opens additional pages for you to specify your target audience and pay for your poll before posting.

To view the results of your polls, click the My Polls tab on the Polls page. On this tab, you can select a poll to view, copy a poll for reuse, or end a poll.

When you click the title link of a poll, LinkedIn displays detailed information about your poll, shown in Figure 13.6.

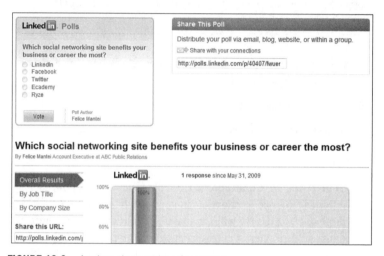

FIGURE 13.6   Analyze the results of your poll.

Here you can

- ► View the total number of responses you've received. Note that each LinkedIn member can vote only once, so no one can skew poll results.

- ► View the response percentage for each potential answer.

- ► View responses by job title and company size.

- ► Share your poll's unique URL with others.

- ► Add and review comments.

To view and respond to polls other LinkedIn members submit, click the Browse Polls tab.

Adding the Reading List by Amazon Application

The Reading List by Amazon application enables you to share book recommendations and reading plans with your LinkedIn connections. LinkedIn installs the Reading List by Amazon application by default.

To add a book to your profile using the Reading List by Amazon application, follow these steps:

1. On the global navigation bar, select Reading List by Amazon on the More drop-down menu. The Reading List by Amazon application opens, with the Network Updates tab selected.

2. In the What Are You Reading section, enter the title of a book you would like to include on your profile.

3. Click the Search Books button to display possible matches. If the book you want to display doesn't appear, revise your search results or search according to author name.

4. Click the Select button below the matching title to continue to the next page (see Figure 13.7).

5. Select one of the following reading options: I Want to Read It, I'm Reading It Now, or I Read It.

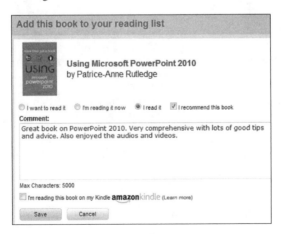

FIGURE 13.7 Share your reading recommendations with your network.

> **TIP: Recommend Books to Your Connections**
>
> If you select the I Read It option button, the I Recommend This Book check box appears. Select this check box if you want to recommend this book to your connections.

6. Enter a comment of up to 5,000 characters. In your comments, explain to your connections why you're including this book and the value it offers.

7. Select the I'm Reading This Book on My Kindle check box if you're reading the Kindle version.

8. Click the Save button to update your reading list.

The book now appears on your profile (see Figure 13.8) and home page (if you selected these display options).

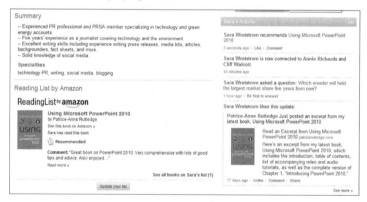

FIGURE 13.8   Your connections can view your reading list on your profile.

To return to this application, select Reading List by Amazon from the More drop-down menu on the global navigation bar. The Network Updates tab is selected by default.

This tab also includes information about the books your connections are reading. For each book that appears, you can click the

▶ Title of the book for more information about the book

▶ See Profile link to view the profile of the person who recommends this book

▶ Watch [First Name]'s List button to add yourself to this person's watch list

▶ Add Book to Your Reading List link to add the book to your own reading list

▶ See This Book on Amazon link to open the book's Amazon page

In addition to the Network Updates tab, the Reading List by Amazon application also includes three other tabs:

▶ **Your Reading List:** Displays a list of all books you added to your reading list. You can edit or delete an existing entry from this list.

▶ **Industry Updates:** Displays books on the reading lists of others in your industry.

▶ **All Recent Updates:** Displays reading list updates from all LinkedIn members.

If you remove the Reading List by Amazon application and want to add it again, follow the steps listed in the "Adding Applications" section earlier in this lesson.

Adding the SlideShare Presentations Application

Using the SlideShare Presentations application, you can embed presentations and other documents from SlideShare (www.slideshare.net), the popular presentation-sharing site. If you don't have an account on SlideShare, you can sign up for one from LinkedIn and start uploading files. The files you choose appear on your profile (see Figure 13.9).

Although SlideShare is best known for sharing presentations such as PowerPoint files, you can also share files of up to 100MB in numerous formats, including Microsoft Word, Microsoft Excel, and PDF. You can also embed YouTube videos in your presentations to give your LinkedIn profile some added flair.

FIGURE 13.9 Use SlideShare to incorporate slideshows into your LinkedIn profile.

To add the SlideShare Presentations application, follow the steps listed in the "Adding Applications" section earlier in this lesson, selecting the SlideShare Presentations application on the Applications page. The SlideShare application opens.

Enter your Username and Password if you already have a SlideShare account and click the Link Existing Profile button. Alternatively, sign up for a SlideShare account and click the Create New Profile button.

The SlideShare application includes the following five tabs.

▶ **Home:** Displays the Network Activity list, detailing the presentations your connections have uploaded. Click the name of any presentation to view it in a player, tweet it on Twitter, share with your connections, add comments, or mark it as a favorite.

▶ **Explore:** Lists the most viewed and most recently uploaded presentations.

▶ **Your Connections:** Displays the presentations your connections have uploaded.

▶ **Your Slidespace:** Offers the following display options: Your Presentations, Your Favorites, or Your Connections. This tab also includes a link to the Settings page where you can specify whether you want to display presentation thumbnails or a complete presentation in a player.

▶ **Upload:** Enables you to upload files to LinkedIn.

Adding the WordPress Application

If you have a WordPress blog, you can display your blog posts on your LinkedIn profile. This application works with both self-hosted WordPress.org blogs and hosted WordPress.com blogs.

TIP: **Also Consider the Blog Link Application**

If you use a solution other than WordPress to host your blog, check out the Blog Link application instead. WordPress users can choose between adding the WordPress application or adding the Blog Link application. Each application performs the same function, but each displays posts in different formats. Refer to the "Adding the Blog Link Application" section earlier in this lesson for more information.

To add the WordPress application, follow these steps:

1. Follow the steps listed in the "Adding Applications" section earlier in this lesson, selecting the WordPress application on the Applications page. The WordPress application opens, shown in Figure 13.10.

FIGURE 13.10   Specify the URL of your WordPress blog.

2. Enter the complete URL of your blog in the text box, such as http://www.patricerutledge.com/blog.

3. Indicate whether you want to show all recent blog posts or only those tagged LinkedIn.

TIP: **You Can Choose to Include Only Selected Blog Posts on LinkedIn**

Tag your blog posts in WordPress with the "linkedin" tag to select which ones you want to appear on LinkedIn.

---

4. Click the Save button to preview your blog posts.

Your WordPress blog posts now appear on your profile and home page (if you selected these display options).

Adding and Managing LinkedIn Events

The LinkedIn Events application enables you to add events to LinkedIn's events calendar, promote events to LinkedIn members, and find events you want to attend. LinkedIn focuses on professional events, both in-person and virtual, rather than personal events.

LinkedIn installs the Events application by default. To open the LinkedIn Events page, select Events from the More drop-down menu on the global navigation bar. This page contains four tabs:

▶ **Events Home:** Browse your connections' events, the most popular events on LinkedIn, and event-related network updates. Click an event's title link to view more details, add comments, and RSVP your participation at the event (such as attending, presenting, exhibiting, or interested). This isn't an official RSVP, but rather a way to let your LinkedIn network know about your event activities. You can also see how many other LinkedIn members RSVPed, including your connections.

▶ **Find Events:** Search for events to attend by keyword, date, location, or event type. Figure 13.11 shows a sample Search Results summary, which also lets you know about your connections' participation.

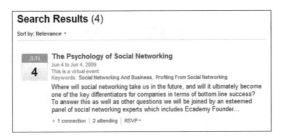

FIGURE 13.11   Use LinkedIn Events to find events to attend and share with your network.

▶ **My Events:** View a list of the events you added or those events for which you submitted an RSVP.

▶ **Add an Event:** Add your own events to the LinkedIn events calendar. Figure 13.12 shows a sample new event.

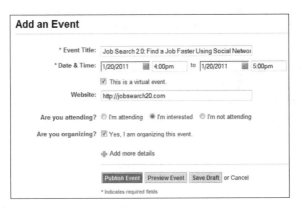

FIGURE 13.12   Add an event and publicize it on LinkedIn.

LinkedIn provides event visibility in its event directory, on member home pages, and member profiles. You can also send a message to your connections about a particular event by clicking the Share link on that event's page. Advertising via LinkedIn DirectAds is another way to promote your event. See Web Lesson 3, "Advertising on LinkedIn," for more information about placing DirectAds.

Removing Applications

Eventually, you might discover that an application isn't as useful as you thought it would be and you want to remove it:

1. On the global navigation bar, select Get More Applications from the More drop-down menu.

2. On the Applications page, click the link for the application you want to remove.

3. In the Application Info box on the right side of the page, click the Remove button.

LinkedIn removes the application from your profile and home page.

You can also update an application's visibility settings from this page. For example, rather than removing an application, you could choose not to display it on your profile or LinkedIn home page.

Summary

In this lesson, you learned how to use LinkedIn applications to enhance your profile and collaborate with your connections.

Using LinkedIn Service Providers

In this lesson, you learn how to locate recommended service providers in the LinkedIn Service Providers directory, make your own recommendations, and request recommendations if you provide professional services.

Understanding LinkedIn Service Providers

The LinkedIn Service Providers feature connects members searching for service providers with members who provide services. If you're searching for a service provider, you can review peer recommendations before hiring. If you provide professional services, you can receive client recommendations and promote your services to prospective buyers through the LinkedIn database of service providers.

> CAUTION: **Understand the Difference Between Recommendation Types**
>
> If you're not a service provider, ask for a colleague or business partner recommendation rather than a service provider recommendation. Refer to Lesson 10, "Requesting and Providing Recommendations," for more information.

LinkedIn offers numerous categories and subcategories of service providers such as Consulting, Employment Services, Financial & Legal Services, and Health & Medical.

Searching for Service Providers

Finding the right service provider is a straightforward process. On the global navigation bar, select Companies from the More drop-down menu. Then click the Service Providers link on the right side of the Companies page. Figure 14.1 illustrates the Service Provider Recommendations page.

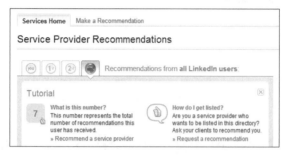

FIGURE 14.1   Learn about the service providers your fellow LinkedIn members recommend.

By default, LinkedIn lists summaries of the most recent recommendations from all members, but you can click the buttons at the top of the page to modify what appears. Options include displaying only your own recommendations, displaying recommendations from 1st degree connections, or displaying recommendations from your 2nd degree network.

> TIP: **Evaluate Recommendations Carefully Before Making Decisions**
>
> Although the LinkedIn Service Providers directory can help you find quality professionals to perform specialized tasks, it's important to analyze recommendations before making a hiring decision. Who are the people making the recommendations? Do the recommendations include valid insight into the provider's performance or are they vague compliments? How many recommendations does a particular provider have? In many cases, the quantity of recommendations is less important than the quality of recommendations.

To search for a specific type of service provider, click the appropriate service category in the Categories box on the right side of the page. LinkedIn narrows the results on the Service Provider Recommendations page to providers in only that category.

If you want to find providers who live in your local area, click the Change Location link. Select a country and optional postal code and click the Change Location button to view providers in that geographic area. Alternatively, you can choose one of the top locations for service providers.

Recommending a Service Provider

To recommend a LinkedIn member who did an outstanding job performing a professional service, follow these steps:

1. On the global navigation bar, select Companies from the More drop-down menu.

2. On the Companies page, click the Service Providers link.

3. Select the Make a Recommendation tab.

4. Click the Select from Your Connections List link to open your connection list in another window.

5. Select the person you want to recommend. LinkedIn returns to the Make a Recommendation tab.

NOTE: **Recommending Someone Who's Not Your Connection**
If you're not connected to the person you want to recommend, enter that person's name and email address. You can even recommend a provider who isn't a LinkedIn member.

6. Click the Continue button. LinkedIn opens the Create Your Recommendation page, shown in Figure 14.2.

7. Select the position you're recommending the person for from the drop-down list. This should be the position associated with the service provider's business.

FIGURE 14.2 Recommend top service providers so that others can find them in LinkedIn's Service Provider directory.

8. Select a Service Category from the drop-down list.

9. In the Year First Hired field, indicate when you first started working with this service provider.

10. If you've worked with this person before, select the I Have Hired [First Name] More Than Once check box.

11. Select up to three attributes for this service provider. LinkedIn allows you to choose only three, so consider carefully which are the most applicable.

12. Enter your recommendation in the text box. Provide specific, concise reasons why you're recommending this person. Vague accolades or short comments like "great guy" don't make effective recommendations. Instead, focus on actual accomplishments and quantifiable achievements. For example, "Ken sold our house in 15 days for more than the asking price" or "Samantha's marketing campaign increased our website traffic by 25%."

13. Click the Send button to send a notification message to the provider that you recommend.

In this message, shown in Figure 14.3, providers can accept the recommendation, request a replacement recommendation, or archive the recommendation for future consideration. Providers also have the choice to display or hide your recommendation on their profile.

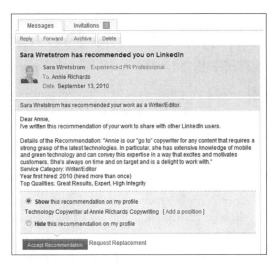

FIGURE 14.3   Providers have the option of accepting or asking for changes on any recommendation they receive.

Figure 14.4 shows a provider profile recommendation.

TIP: **Edit or Withdraw a Service Provider Recommendation**

You can edit or withdraw (delete) a service provider recommendation just as you can any other recommendation. On the global navigation bar, select Recommendations from the Profile drop-down menu and then select the Sent Recommendations tab to make your changes. Refer to Lesson 10 for more information.

FIGURE 14.4   Providers can display recommendations for their connections—and potential clients—to see.

Requesting a Service Provider Recommendation

If you're a service provider, you don't need to wait for a client to submit a recommendation for you. You can ask for one by following these steps:

1. On the global navigation bar, select Companies from the More drop-down menu.

2. On the Companies page, click the Service Providers link.

3. On the Service Provider Recommendations page, click the Request a Recommendation link. Figure 14.5 shows the Request Recommendations page.

4. In step 1, choose the position for which you want the recommendation from the drop-down list. This should be the job associated with your work as a service provider.

5. In step 2, select connections to ask for a recommendation. Click the View All Connections icon to select from a list of your connections. Although you can contact up to 200 connections, it's a much better practice to contact one person at a time and customize your request.

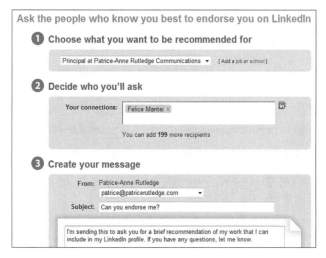

FIGURE 14.5 Request a recommendation to gain visibility in the Service Providers directory.

6. When you're finished selecting connections, click the Finished button to return to the Request Recommendations page.

7. In step 3, you can use the sample text LinkedIn provides or, preferably, replace it with a personalized message.

8. Click the Send button to send your recommendation request for completion and approval.

Read "Responding to a Service Provider Recommendation Request," later in this lesson, to learn more about what happens after you send your request.

TIP: **Specify That You Want a Service Provider Recommendation**

Because a recommender can provide three types of recommendations, be sure to ask for a service provider recommendation.

Responding to a Service Provider Recommendation Request

When someone requests a service provider recommendation from you, LinkedIn sends a message with "Can You Endorse Me?" as the default subject line.

If you want to provide a recommendation, follow these steps:

1. Click the subject line to open the recommendation request.

2. Click the Write Recommendation button to open the Select Type page.

3. Select Service Provider as the recommendation type you want to write.

4. Click the Continue button to open the Create Your Recommendation page. The fields on this page are the same whether you take the initiative to create a service provider recommendation or respond to a request for one. Refer to "Recommending a Service Provider," earlier in this lesson, for details about how to complete this page.

Summary

In this lesson, you learned how to find recommended service providers and how to receive recommendations if you provide professional services.

CHAPTER 15

Using LinkedIn Mobile

Learn how to keep up with LinkedIn using your mobile phone.

Using LinkedIn Mobile

LinkedIn Mobile enables you to view selected LinkedIn data and perform selected LinkedIn tasks on your mobile phone. If you use a BlackBerry, iPhone, or Palm, you should also consider the LinkedIn application specific to your phone.

To learn more about LinkedIn Mobile options, click the Mobile link on the bottom navigation menu.

Accessing LinkedIn on Your Mobile Phone

With LinkedIn Mobile, you can access LinkedIn on any mobile phone with Internet access.

To access LinkedIn on your mobile phone, follow these steps:

1. Point to http://m.linkedin.com.

2. Enter your email address and LinkedIn password.

3. Click the Sign In button.

4. Choose from the following options:

   ▶ **0 Search:** Search by keywords, name, company, or title.

▶ **1 Updates:** Update your status or view network updates of your connections.

▶ **2 Contacts:** View summaries of your connections with links to their profiles and email.

▶ **3 Profile:** View your profile.

▶ **4 Invite:** Invite people to connect with you on LinkedIn.

▶ **5 Settings:** Select your preferred language. Choices include English, German, Spanish, French, Japanese, or Chinese (either traditional or simplified).

▶ **6 Feedback:** Provide feedback to LinkedIn.

▶ **7 Sign Out:** Sign out of LinkedIn.

Figure 15.1 shows a sample profile using LinkedIn Mobile. The way LinkedIn Mobile appears on your phone varies by manufacturer.

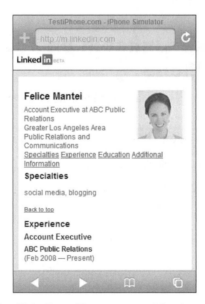

FIGURE 15.1　View LinkedIn profiles on your mobile phone.

Using the LinkedIn iPhone Application

LinkedIn offers a free application for the iPhone that's compatible with the iPod Touch and iPad and integrates with your iPhone address book. This application requires iPhone OS 3.0 or later. It's available in English, Chinese, French, German, Italian, Japanese, Portuguese, and Spanish.

Figure 15.2 shows network updates on the iPhone.

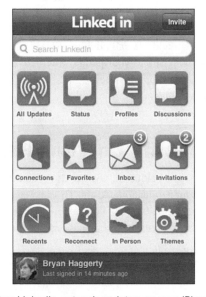

FIGURE 15.2   View LinkedIn network updates on your iPhone.

To download this application, click the Mobile link on the bottom navigation menu, and then click the iPhone link on the LinkedIn Mobile page. Alternatively, search the App Store in iTunes.

Using LinkedIn on Your BlackBerry

LinkedIn for BlackBerry enables you to work with your BlackBerry contacts, calendar, and messaging. This application is available for Tour, Bold, Curve, Storm, and Pearl using OS 4.3.0 or higher.

To download LinkedIn for BlackBerry, follow these steps:

1. On the bottom navigation menu, click the Mobile link.

2. On the LinkedIn Mobile page, click the BlackBerry link.

3. Click the Get It Now button.

4. Enter your email address and click the Send Email button to email a download link to your phone. Alternatively, type the following link on your BlackBerry: http://m.linkedin.com/blackberry/download.

Using LinkedIn on Your Palm

If you own a Palm Pre or Palm Pixi, you can download the free LinkedIn application in the Palm application catalog. This app enables you to search and view profiles, send email to your connections, send invitations to connect, and view and accept outstanding invitations.

To download, click the Mobile link on the bottom navigation menu and then click the Palm link on the LinkedIn Mobile page.

Summary

In this lesson, you learned how to access LinkedIn from your mobile phone and download device-specific LinkedIn mobile applications.

Index

SamsTeachYourself

from Sams Publishing

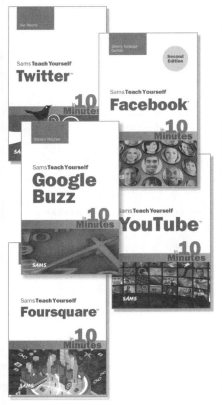

Sams **Teach Yourself in 10 Minutes**
offers straightforward, practical answers
for fast results.

These small books of 250 pages or less
offer tips that point out shortcuts and
solutions, cautions that help you avoid
common pitfalls, and notes that explain
additional concepts and provide additional
information. By working through the
10-minute lessons, you learn everything
you need to know quickly and easily!

When you only have time for the answers,
Sams Teach Yourself books are your
best solution.

Visit **informit.com/samsteachyourself**
for a complete listing of the products
available.

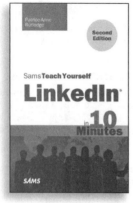

FREE Online Edition

Your purchase of **Sams Teach Yourself LinkedIn in 10 Minutes** includes access to a free online edition for 45 days through the Safari Books Online subscription service. Nearly every Sams book is available online through Safari Books Online, along with more than 5,000 other technical books and videos from publishers such as Addison-Wesley Professional, Cisco Press, Exam Cram, IBM Press, O'Reilly, Prentice Hall, and Que.

SAFARI BOOKS ONLINE allows you to search for a specific answer, cut and paste code, download chapters, and stay current with emerging technologies.

Activate your FREE Online Edition at www.informit.com/safarifree

> **STEP 1:** Enter the coupon code: TCAKYFA.

> **STEP 2:** New Safari users, complete the brief registration form. Safari subscribers, just log in.

If you have difficulty registering on Safari or accessing the online edition, please e-mail customer-service@safaribooksonline.com

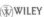